MW01453628

A Collection of Sermons

Comforting a Nation

A Collection of Sermons Delivered After the Assassination of Abraham Lincoln

By
Larry A Toller

"Comforting a Nation" by Larry A. Toller
Copyright © 2015 by Larry Toller
A SecondWind Publication
All rights reserved.

ISBN-13: 978-1-312-88800-5
All graphics, photos and Sermons are in the public domain.
(www.archive.org) Library of Congress

A Collection of Sermons

Table of Contents

Introduction 5

Dr. Phineas D. Gurley,
Pastor to the President
Funeral April 19, 1865 6

Rev. M. F. Gaddis
April 16, 1865 23

Rev. John Falkner Blake
April 16, 1865 47

Rev. A. D. Mayo
April 16, 1865 73

Rev. Henry E. Parker
April 16, 1865 116

Rev. Cephas B. Crane
April 16, 1865 131

Rev. George D. Boardman
April 19, 1865 155

Rev. Matthew Simpson
The burial May 4, 1865 170

INTRODUCTION

President Abraham Lincoln was assassinated on Good Friday, April 12, 1865. As the news spread across the nation, pastors knew their Easter Sunday message must change. The nation was plunged into mourning and as they entered places of worship on Sunday, they needed a Word from the Lord. They needed comfort. Many sermons and orations marked the occasion of President Lincoln's death on April 14, 1865. Among the most famous is the sermon delivered at Lincoln's funeral, held at the Executive Mansion in Washington, D.C. on the nineteenth of April, by Reverend Phineas Gurley (1816-1868). These sermons by prominent Pastors of the day are representative of multitudes who brought comfort to a grieving nation.

A COLLECTION OF SERMONS

DR. PHINEAS D. GURLEY, PASTOR TO THE PRESIDENT FUNERAL APRIL 19, 1865

Dr. Gurney, pastor of the New York Avenue Presbyterian Church, which Abraham Lincoln attended while President, preached this funeral sermon in the White House East Room.

The Rev. Dr. Phineas Gurley, pastor of NYAPC, 1860-1868, was a spiritual advisor to Abraham Lincoln

Dr. Gurley was at Lincoln's side when he died four days earlier and rode the Lincoln funeral train to Springfield, Illinois, where he concluded the burial service with prayer. The sermon is a powerful effort, revealing how the Lincoln family pastor viewed the President's position in history.

Comforting a Nation

Copy of photo by Alexander Gardner taken at Gardner's Gallery in Washington, DC, on Sunday, February 5, 1865. This last photo in Lincoln's last photo session from life was long thought to have been made on April 10, 1865, but more recent research has indicated the earlier date in February. The original surviving print is at the National Portrait Gallery.[L]

A Collection of Sermons

Faith in God:
A Sermon

Delivered in the East Room of the Executive Mansion,

Wednesday April 19th, 1865,

At

The Funeral of Abraham Lincoln, President of the U. States

By

The Rev. P. D. Gurley, D. D.,
Pastor of the New York Avenue Presbyterian Church,
Washington,
D. C.

The Funeral

AS WE STAND HERE TODAY, MOURNERS AROUND THIS COFFIN AND AROUND THE LIFELESS REMAINS OF OUR BELOVED CHIEF MAGISTRATE, WE RECOGNIZE AND WE ADORE THE SOVEREIGNTY OF GOD. His throne is in the heavens, and His kingdom ruleth over all. He hath done, and He hath permitted to be done, whatsoever He pleased. "Clouds and darkness are round about Him; righteousness and judgment are the habitation of His throne." His way is in the sea, and His path in the great waters, and His footsteps are not known. "Canst thou by searching find out God? Canst thou find out the Almighty unto perfection? It is as high as heaven; what canst thou do? Deeper than hell; what canst thou know? The measure thereof is longer than the earth, and broader than the sea. If He cut off, and shut up, or gather together, then who can hinder Him? For He knoweth vain men; he seeth wickedness also; will He not then consider it?"-- We bow before His infinite majesty. We bow, we weep, we worship.

> "Where reason fails, with all her powers,
> There faith prevails, and love adores."

It was a cruel, cruel hand, that dark hand of the assassin, which smote our honored, wise, and noble President, and filled the land with sorrow. But above and beyond that hand there is another, which we must see and acknowledge. It is the chastening hand of a wise and a faithful Father. He gives us this bitter cup. And the cup that our Father hath given us, shall we not drink it?

> God of the just, Thou gavest us the cup:
> We yield to thy behest, and drink it up."
> "Whom the Lord loveth He chasteneth."

O how these blessed words have cheered and strengthened and sustained us through all these long and weary years of civil strife, while our friends and brothers on so many ensanguined fields were falling and dying for the cause of Liberty and Union! Let them cheer, and strengthen, and sustain us today.

True, this new sorrow and chastening has come in such an hour and in such a way as we thought not, and it bears the impress of a rod that is very heavy, and of a mystery that is very deep. That such a life should be sacrificed, at such a time, by such a foul and diabolical agency; that the man at the head of the nation, whom the people had learned to trust with a confiding and a loving confidence, and upon whom more than upon any other were centered, under God, our best hopes for the true and speedy pacification of the country, the restoration of the Union, and the return of harmony and love; that he should be taken from us, and taken just as the prospect of peace was brightly opening upon our torn and bleeding country, and just as he was beginning to be animated and gladdened with the hope of ere long enjoying with the people the blessed fruit and reward of his and their toil, and care, and patience, and self-sacrificing devotion to the interests of Liberty and the Union--O it is a mysterious and a most afflicting visitation!

But it is our Father in heaven, the God of our fathers, and our God, who permits us to be so suddenly and sorely smitten; and we know that His judgments are right, and that in faithfulness He has afflicted us. In the midst of our rejoicings we needed this stroke, this dealing, this discipline; and therefore He has sent it.

Let us remember, our affliction has not come forth out of the dust, and our trouble has not sprung out of the ground. Through and beyond all second causes let us look, and see the sovereign permissive agency of the great First Cause. It is His prerogative to bring light out of darkness and good out of evil. Surely the wrath of man shall praise Him, and the remainder of wrath He will restrain. In the light of a clearer day we may yet see that the wrath which planned and perpetuated the death of the President, was overruled by Him whose judgments are unsearchable, and His ways are past finding out, for the highest welfare of all those interests which are so dear to the Christian patriot and philanthropist, and for which a loyal people have made such an unexampled sacrifice of treasure and of blood. Let us not be faithless, but believing.

> "Blind unbelief is prone to err,
> And scan His work in vain;
> God is his own interpreter,
> And He will make it plain."

We will wait for his interpretation, and we will wait in faith, nothing doubting. He who has led us so well, and defended and prospered us so wonderfully during the last four years of toil, and struggle, and sorrow, will not forsake us now. He may chasten, but He will not destroy. He may purify us more and more in the furnace of trial, but He will not consume us. No, no! He has chosen us as He did his people of old in the furnace of affliction, and He has said of us as He said of them, "This people have I formed for myself; they shall show forth my praise."

Let our principal anxiety now be that this new sorrow may be a sanctified sorrow; that it may lead us to deeper repentance, to a more humbling sense of our dependence upon God, and to the more unreserved consecration of ourselves and all that we have to the cause of truth and justice, of law and order, of liberty and good government, of pure and undefiled religion.

Then, though weeping may endure for a night, joy will come in the morning. Blessed be God! Despite of this great and sudden and temporary darkness, the morning has begun to dawn--the morning of a bright and glorious day, such as our country has never seen. That day will come and not tarry, and the death of an hundred Presidents and their Cabinets can never, never prevent it. While we are thus hopeful, however, let us also be humble.

The occasion calls us to prayerful and tearful humiliation. It demands of us that we lie low, very low, before Him who has smitten us for our sins. O that all our rulers and all our people may bow in the dust today beneath the chastening hand of God! And may their voices go up to Him as one voice, and their hearts go up to Him as one heart, pleading with Him for mercy, for grace to sanctify our great and sore bereavement, and for wisdom to guide us in this our time of need. Such a united cry and pleading will not be in vain. It will enter into the ear and heart of Him who sits upon the throne, and He will say to us, as to His ancient Israel, "In a little wrath I hid my face from thee for a moment: but with everlasting kindness will I have mercy upon thee, saith the Lord, thy Redeemer."

I have said that the people confided in the late lamented President with a full and a loving confidence. Probably no man since the days of Washington was ever so deeply and firmly embedded and enshrined in the very hearts of the people as Abraham Lincoln. Nor was it a mistaken confidence and love. He deserved it well--deserved it all. He merited it by his character, by his acts, and by the whole tenor, and tone, and spirit of his life. He was simple and sincere, plain and honest, truthful and just, benevolent and kind. His perceptions were quick and clear, his judgments were calm and accurate, and his purposes were good and pure beyond a question. Always and everywhere he aimed and endeavored to be right and to do right. His integrity was thorough, all pervading, all controlling, and incorruptible. It was the same in every place and relation, in the consideration and the control of matters great or small, the same firm and steady principle of power and beauty that shed a clear and crowning luster upon all his other excellences of mind and heart, and recommended him to his fellow citizens as the man, who, in a time of unexampled peril, when the very life of the nation was at stake, should be chosen to occupy, in the country and for the country, its highest post of power and responsibility. How wisely and well, how purely and faithfully, how firmly and steadily, how justly and successfully he did occupy that post and meet its grave demands in circumstances of surpassing trial and difficulty, is known to you all, known to the country and the world.

He comprehended from the first the perils to which treason has exposed the freest and best Government on the earth, the vast interests of Liberty and humanity that were to be saved or lost forever in the urgent impending conflict; he rose to the dignity and momentousness of the occasion, saw his duty as the Chief Magistrate of a great and imperiled people, and he determined to do his duty, and his whole duty, seeking the guidance and leaning upon the arm of Him of whom it is written, "He giveth power to the faint, and to them that have no might He increaseth strength." Yes, he leaned upon His arm. He recognized and received the truth that the "kingdom is the Lord's, and He is the governor among the nations." He remembered that "God is in history," and he felt that nowhere had His hand and His mercy been so marvelously conspicuous as in the history of this nation. He hoped and he prayed that that same hand would continue to guide us, and that same mercy continue to abound to us in the time of our greatest need.

I speak what I know, and testify what I have often heard him say, when I affirm that that guidance and mercy were the props on which he humbly and habitually leaned; they were the best hope he had for himself and for his country. Hence, when he was leaving his home in Illinois, and coming to this city to take his seat in the executive chair of a disturbed and troubled nation, he said to the old and tried friends who gathered tearfully around him and bade him farewell, "I leave you with this request: pray for me." They did pray for him; and millions of other people prayed for him; nor did they pray in vain. Their prayer was heard, and the answer appears in all his subsequent history; it shines forth with a heavenly radiance in the whole course and tenor of his administration, from its commencement to its close. God raised him up for a great and glorious mission, furnished him for his work, and aided him in its accomplishment. Nor was it merely by strength of mind, and honesty of heart, and purity and pertinacity of purpose, that He furnished him; in addition to these things, He gave him a calm and abiding confidence in the overruling providence of God and in the ultimate triumph of truth and righteousness through the power and the blessing of God.

This confidence strengthened him in all his hours of anxiety and toil, and inspired him with calm and cheering hope when others were inclining to despondency and gloom. Never shall I forget the emphasis and the deep emotion with which he said in this very room, to a company of clergymen and others, who called to pay him their respects in the darkest days of our civil conflict: "Gentlemen, my hope of success in this great and terrible struggle rests on that immutable foundation, the justice and goodness of God. And when events are very threatening, and prospects very dark, I still hope that in some way which man can not see all will be well in the end, because our cause is just, and God is on our side." Such was his sublime and holy faith, and it was an anchor to his soul, both sure and steadfast. It made him firm and strong. It emboldened him in the pathway of duty, however rugged and perilous it might be. It made him valiant for the right; for the cause of God and humanity, and it held him in a steady, patient, and unswerving adherence to a policy of administration which he thought, and which we all now think, both God and humanity required him to adopt. We admired and loved him on many accounts--for strong and various reasons: we admired his childlike simplicity, his freedom from guile and deceit, his staunch and sterling integrity, his kind and forgiving temper, his industry and patience, his persistent, self-sacrificing devotion to all the duties of his eminent position, from the least to the greatest; his readiness to hear and consider the cause of the poor and humble, the suffering and the oppressed; his charity toward those who questioned the correctness of his opinions and the wisdom of his policy; his wonderful skill in reconciling differences among the friends of the Union, leading them away from abstractions, and inducing them to work together and harmoniously for the common weal; his true and enlarged philanthropy, that knew no distinction of color or race, but regarded all men as brethren, and endowed alike by their Creator "with certain inalienable rights, among which are life, Liberty, and the pursuit of happiness"; his inflexible purpose that what freedom had gained in our terrible civil strife should never be lost, and that the end of the war should be the end of slavery, and, as a consequence, of rebellion; his readiness to spend and be spent for the attainment of such a triumph--a triumph, the blessed fruits of which shall be as wide spreading as the earth and as enduring as the sun:--all these things commanded and fixed our admiration and the admiration of the world, and stamped upon his character and life the unmistakable impress of greatness. But more sublime than any or all of these, more holy and influential, more beautiful, and strong, and sustaining, was his abiding confidence in God and in the final triumph of truth and righteousness through Him and for His is sake.

This was his noblest virtue, his grandest principle, the secret alike of his strength, his patience, and his success. And this, it seems to me, after being near him steadily, and with him often, for more than four years, is the principle by which, more than by any other, "he, being dead, yet speaketh." Yes; by his steady enduring confidence in God, and in the complete ultimate success of the cause of God, which is the cause of humanity, more than by any other way, does he now speak to us and to the nation he loved and served so well. By this he speaks to his successor in office, and charges him to " have faith in God." By this he speaks to the members of his cabinet, the men with whom he counseled so often and was associated so long, and he charges them to "have faith in Cod." By this he speaks to the officers and men of our noble army and navy, and, as they stand at their posts of duty and peril, he charges them to "have faith in God." By this he speaks to all who occupy positions of influence and authority in these sad and troublous times, and he charges them all to "have faith in God." By this he speaks to this great people as they sit in sackcloth today, and weep for him with a bitter wailing, and refuse to be comforted, and he charges them to "have faith in God." And by this he will speak through the ages and to all rulers and peoples in every land, and his message to them will be, "Cling to Liberty and right; battle for them; bleed for them; die for them, if need be; and have confidence in God." O that the voice of this testimony may sink down into our hearts today and every day, and into the heart of the nation, and exert its appropriate influence upon our feelings, our faith, our patience, and our devotion to the cause of freedom and humanity-a cause dearer to us now than ever before, because consecrated by the blood of its most conspicuous defender, its wisest and most fondly-trusted friend. He is dead; but the God in whom he trusted lives, and He can guide and strengthen his successor, as He guided and strengthened him. He is dead; but the memory of his virtues, of his wise and patriotic counsels and labors, of his calm and steady faith in God lives, is precious, and will be a power for good in the country quite down to the end of time. He is dead; but the cause he so ardently loved, so ably, patiently. Faithfully represented and defended-not for himself only. Not for us only, but for all people in all their coming generations, till time shall be no more- that cause survives his fall, and will survive it. The light of its brightening prospects flashes cheeringly today athwart the gloom occasioned by his death, and the language of God's united providences is telling us that, though the friends of Liberty die, Liberty itself is immortal. There is no assassin strong enough and no weapon deadly enough to quench its inextinguishable life, or arrest its onward march to the conquest and empire of the world. This is our confidence, and this is our consolation, as we weep and mourn today. Though our beloved President is slain, our beloved country is saved. And so we sing of mercy as well as of judgment. Tears of gratitude mingle with those of sorrow. While there is darkness, there is also the dawning of a brighter, happier day upon our stricken and weary land. God be praised that our fallen Chief lived long enough to see the day dawn and the daystar of joy and peace arise upon the nation. He saw it, and he was glad. Alas! Alas! He only saw the dawn, when the sun has risen, . . . glorious, and a happy reunited people are rejoicing in its light,-alas! alas! It will shine upon his grave. But that grave will be a precious and a consecrated spot. The friends of Liberty and of the Union will repair to it in years and ages to come, to pronounce the memory of its occupant blessed, and, gathering from his very ashes, and from the rehearsal of his deeds and virtues, fresh incentives to patriotism, they will there renew their vows of fidelity to their country and their God.

And now I know not that I can more appropriately conclude this discourse, which is but a sincere and simple utterance of the heart, than by addressing to our departed President, with some slight modification, the language which Tacitus, in his life of Agricola, addresses to his venerable and departed father-in-law: "With you we may now congratulate; you are blessed, not only because your life was a career of glory, but because you were released, when, your country safe, it was happiness to die. We have lost a parent, and, in our distress, it is now an addition to our heartfelt sorrow that we had it not in our power to commune with FAITH IN GOD you on the bed of languishing, and receive your last embrace.

Your dying words would have been ever dear to us; your commands we should have treasured up, and graved them on our hearts. This sad comfort we have lost, and the wound for that reason, pierces deeper. From the world of spirits behold your disconsolate family and people; exalt our minds from fond regret and unavailing grief to contemplation of your virtues. Those we must not lament; it was impiety to sully them with a tear. To cherish their memory, to embalm them with our praises, and, so far as we can, to emulate your bright example, will be the truest mark of our respect, the best tribute we can offer.

Your wife will thus preserve the memory of the best of husbands, and thus your children will prove their filial piety. By dwelling constantly on your words and actions, they will have an illustrious character before their eyes, and, not content with the bare image of your mortal frame, they will have what is more valuable-the form and features of your mind. Busts and statues, like their originals, are frail and perishable. The soul is formed of finer elements, and its inward form is not to be expressed by the hand of an artist with unconscious matter-our manners and our morals may in some degree trace the resemblance. All of you that gained our love and raised our admiration still subsists, and will ever subsist, preserved in the minds of men, the register of ages, and the records of fame. Others, who had figured on the stage of life and were the worthies of a former day, will sink, for want of a faithful historian, into the common lot of oblivion, inglorious and unremembered; but you, our lamented friend and head, delineated with truth, and fairly consigned to posterity, will survive yourself, and triumph over the injuries of time."

Rev. M. F. Gaddis
April 16, 1865

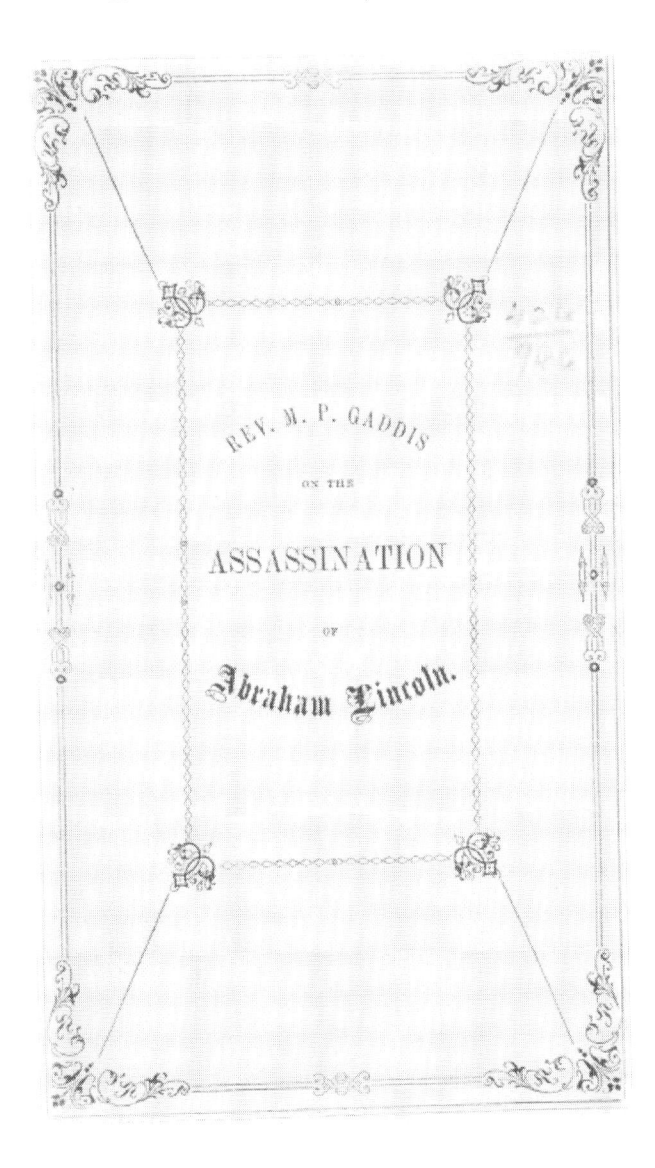

A Collection of Sermons

THE DEATH OF THE PRESIDENT.

The following scenes, descriptive of the excitement attending the delivery of Mr. Gaddis' sermon, is taken from the Cincinnati Daily Times, Monday, April 18th:

Long before dark, Sunday evening, an immense crowd congregated in front of the Methodist Church, on Sixth Street, between Vine and Eace, presided over by Rev. M. F. Gaddis. No sooner had the doors been thrown open, than the crowd immediately filled the church to overflowing, but not one-fourth of the crowd could get in, and thousands remained outside, filling up all the approaches to it; and when the time came for the pastor to open the services, he found it n matter of impossibility to do so, as he could not even got an entrance to the church. Finding it impossible to proceed with the services in his church, a committee of several of our well known citizens, having procured the consent of Mr. Gaddis to deliver his sermon in Mozart Hall, providing that Hall could be obtained, an announcement was immediately made from the church steps, of the intention to deliver the sermon from that place, but some delay would take place, as the janitor would have to be seen, and the Hall lighted.

The crowd immediately proceeded to Mozart Hall, and waited there patiently for it to be opened. Some disappointment was manifested when it was found that the Hall could not be obtained, the janitor refusing the use of it, as his orders were not to let the Hall that evening for any purpose. Another announcement was then made, that as it was then late, and even if the Opera House could be procured, it would take at least an hour before the house could be lighted, it would be impossible to carry the idea into effect, and that Mr. Gaddis would be compelled to deliver his sermon in his church to as many as were fortunate enough to crowd into it. The immense crowd then left Mozart Hall, and proceeded back to the church, which was soon crowded to overflowing, but thousands still remained outside, and showed no disposition to leave the vicinity, not only the sidewalks being full, but the street also. It seems, however, that the committee were not to be deterred from their efforts to obtain a hall, and finally were successful in procuring the Opera House, and the announcement being made to the crowd, it moved for Fourth street, hundreds of ladies and gentlemen hurrying through the streets on the double-quick, for fear they would not get there in time.

It was but a few minutes, and the crowd in front of the Opera House numbered its thousands — the sidewalks and streets soon being full of an anxious, excited multitude. A few minutes transpired, and the doors were open, and the crowd commenced pressing its way in without regard to order. Ladies fainted away, bonnets were smashed in, dresses were torn, but the crowd squeezed, they jammed and rammed, but they determined to get into the Opera House. But in this they utterly failed. Notwithstanding the Opera House was filled to overflowing, the isles being filled, and every nook and corner of it crowded to its utmost capacity, yet hundreds had to go away without finding even standing room.

We have seen crowds in our time, and have seen them in the Opera House, but we think this would beat them all. We certainly never have seen a larger, or more attentive and orderly audience, than on this occasion.

Rev. Mr. Gaddis was received with great applause. He opened the services by some very appropriate remarks; to the effect that he had prepared this sermon for his church, and that he was greatly surprised at the turn affairs had taken, and hoped the audience would take into consideration all the circumstances of the occasion. He then gave out the hymn, and requested the audience to join in singing it:

"Oh, for a thousand tongues to sing Our great Redeemer's praise: The glories of our God and King, The triumphs of his grace."

Mr. Gaddis, in opening, remarked that on Friday last he took occasion in his thanksgiving sermon to say, that now was the time for a great people, in the face of one of the grandest triumphs achieved by any people, to show a magnanimity to their conquered enemies, equal to their triumphs, but since the tragic scenes of the past few hours, resulting in the death of the Chieftain of all these victories, the sermon on the present occasion would materially differ in its sentiments from the one referred to.

He selected for his text the 3d chapter of second Samuel, in which is recorded the assassination of Abner, Captain General of the Israelites, confining his remarks in the main to the 38th verse : " Know ye not that a Prince and a great man has fallen this day in Israel." As remarked above, Mr. Gaddis had prepared his discourse for his own congregation, not aware that he was to deliver it in the finest hall in America, to over four thousand people. Below we give the contents of the sermon as we were enabled to obtain it.

THE SERMON
In looking at the sad events of the past few hours, I can but say in the language of the poet —
> "God moves in a mysterious way, His wonders to perform; lie plants His footsteps in the sea, And rides upon the storm."

And, as on this sorrowful day — a day fraught with more grief than all others in the history of this rebellion—I behold the sorrow and anguish that rends the hearts of a grateful, liberty-loving people, I continue to sing —

" Judge not the Lord by feeble sense, But trust Him to His grace — Behind this frowning providence, lfe hides a smiling face."

As for grief, we have, during the past four years, become inured to its stings. The wails of early widowhood, the sighs of orphanage, the falling of paternal and fraternal tears over the graves, biers, and memories of our loved ones, have not only freighted northern, but southern gales—filling the entire land with sadness, giving us naught but a daily continuation of terrible facts.

The sun of the 11th of April, 1865, rose in unclouded splendor, and shone upon millions of freemen ready to join in the festivities and thanksgivings that were to take place over the triumphs of our armies; — it set only to rise again upon one of the most terrible tragedies ever enacted since the race of man began — set amid a blaze of glory and joy to rise upon the nation clad in the habiliments of grief and shame — grief over the loss of a great and good man, and shame over the fact that an American struck the terrible blow. E'en now there comes up from the capital of our country a wail of anguish, penetrating every vein and artery of the nation — one more keen in its cuttings than all the rest combined; nay, more, the stroke is so piercing that it tears open every wound made in the body of Liberty since the war began, starts fresh fountains of tears from the weeping bereaved ones of the land, and almost opens again the graves of our dead braves. The wild refrain of this wail is, "Abraham Lincoln is dead!"

My hearers, do you realize the deep significance of those words, "Abraham Lincoln is dead?" The most natural question upon an announcement like this is, "And how did he die?" In the quietude of his own chamber, with his family around him, after the great mission of his glorious life was accomplished? "Was it amid the bright light of the peace he sought to bring to the nation over which he presided, and to whose interest he gave the full strength of his manhood? Had he just finished writing some proclamation that was to give liberty to millions of the human family, or teaching the world some grand lesson in the terse, simple expressions of "To whom it may concern?"

Was it while he was engaged in giving expression to the mercy that flowed from a heart overcharged with the same, in the shape of a general amnesty to repentant rebels? Was it at a time when the ship of State was struggling amid the mad waves of the rebellion, with the desired haven of peace still hidden from his sight?" No; — all this, thank God, was accomplished ere the fiendish deed was done.

The proclamation was not only written, but the chains had fallen, under its power, from over throe millions of enslaved men, "To whom it may concern " had gone forth to the worm, and has in the past and is today accomplishing its mission. His last great act of mercy had been written, and the Amnesty read even in the streets of the Eebel capital! The ship of State was no longer in the maelstrom of rebellion. The shoals and quicksands were passed, the destined haven of peace was in view, and the anchor was being thrown overboard to find a fastening from which it was never more to be loosed. Its enemies were conquered, its millions of passengers were happy, its thousands of hardy sailors and defenders were preparing to taste again the joys of home. Its pilot came out from his place of watching and trial, to gratify a grateful people by his presence, when, from some unseen hold of treason, there sprang up a Rebel sailor, a hater of the proclamations, a non-submissionist to whom it may concern, a despiser of mercy, and who, amid the storm, tried to scuttle the ship, dismantle its shrouds, or run it upon the destructive rocks of northern sympathy, and with a cowardly heart, and still more cowardly design, took the life of the great pilot.

Thus fell Abraham Lincoln, President of these United States. Fell as he lived, seeking to make his fellow men happy; fell, too, by the hands of those who had the best reasons for regarding him as their truest friend: for in the midst of his successful efforts to preserve the government he had sworn to protect, he, at the same time, tempered the winds of vengeance to the meanest of its foes.

Some one has said, "Caesar was merciful; Scipio was content; Hannibal was patient, and that George Washington combined these in one;" but yet it is not said of them, as the world must now say of the great departed, "he loved his enemies."

Like him of old, who came to subdue the rebellion of earth against the government of God, he died, saying, "Father, forgive them, they know not what they do."

Looking upon Mr. Lincoln in this light, may we not, with great propriety, say, as does David in the text, "Know ye not that there is a Prince, and a great man fallen this day in Israel" — and with equal propriety adopt the same writer's language as given in the context, "I and my kingdom are guiltless before the Lord forever from the blood of Abner." Are we all innocent? Can we all say that there is no drop of Mr. Lincoln's blood on our skirts? I am afraid that there are some here in our own city that will, in the Day of Judgment, find at least one drop of Mr. Lincoln's blood upon their skirts. Then turning from this declaration of our innocence, after having extended the hand of forgiveness to them as we did on Friday last, to find it so treacherously and horribly spurned, may we not call clown David's curses upon the murderer, as he did on the head of the assassin Joab? I do not desire to take God's work in my unholy hands, for he has said, "Vengeance is mine; I will repay." I am willing to leave the penalty with dim; for if ever God loved any man he must have loved Abraham Lincoln, and ho stands pledged to avenge his own. In this I rest satisfied, for His pledges are immutable. Feeling, then, that there have been times in the administrations of God's government when vengeance was necessary, I pray him now, in view of the great crime just committed — committed, too, in the name of liberty-— that all the curses pronounced by David against Joab for the murder of Abner, may befall the murderer of our President: "May the results of his perfidious act rest upon his head, and on all his father's house; and let there not fail from the house of Joab one that hath an issue, or that is a leper, or that leaneth on a staff, or that falleth on a sword, or that lacketh bread."

And may we, who feel so deeply this treasonable work, live to see the time when, out of this darkness, there shall come glory and honor to all those who loved the victim, and hated the murderer. It is not my purpose, at this time, to enter upon a history of the life and services of Mr. Lincoln. He needs no written or spoken history. His memory, the glory and goodness of his deeds, are written on an imperishable tablet: on the heart of liberty-loving humanity wherever it breathes the air of freedom, or tramples upon broken shackles; nay more, it will cheer the hope of those of our race who are still oppressed, until the morn of their redemption comes, and with it the fulfillment of that song of universal freedom, that came first from Heaven, and will not return again until earth returns with it, to Eden and God.

He has gone from us. And while I would not wipe away a single tear that falls from millions of eyes to-night, or check one of the unnumbered sighs' that come up from as many wailing hearts, allow me to say that our tears and our sighs will not call him back. His place is vacant forever; his mantle falls upon the shoulders of others. This being the case, let us look backward over his illustrious life for consolation, and forward to the great results that must flow, not only to us as a nation, but to the world at large, from his tragic death. I shall attempt no eulogy — I am not equal to the task. His own life, as we know it, constitutes his best eulogy. Neither shall I attempt to apologize for God in his actions toward us as a nation. Had we loved and served him as He has loved and served us, there would have been no occasion, in the administering of his wise Providence, for the removal of the President. I look away from our sorrow to-night; I look up from that small house, that now contains all that is left of earth, to the God of all good — to Him who gave us such a President— to find his countenance smiling in mercy upon us. I hear him say that all these things shall work together for our good. God alone can estimate the value of liberty; hence he gave us Mr. Lincoln, in order to enhance its value in our eyes, and then took him away that its newly developed glories, as connected with his memory, might become still more precious to us. The value of a blessing in this world is generally estimated by its cost. In this view of the subject the blessings of civil liberty should be dearer to us now than all else, save the consolations of our holy religion, and this in our hearts only makes its blessings more sweet. It took over four thousand years of sacrifice and offering upon the altars of God, and ultimately the death of his own son, to redeem man from sin. into the pleasant liberty of righteousness; and the marks of this mighty struggle arc traceable in blood from where Abel offered his bleeding victim down to Calvary's summit, where, through the blood of Jesus, victory came and Satan was conquered. The price paid for liberty stands next to this. I have not time to trace its struggles, its defeats or victories, or to show how near its triumph is complete. Its history, as connected with our own fair land, will be sufficient to show you the immense and, may I say, the dreadful price to be paid for its blessings. Head o'er the struggles of our forefathers, from their landing on the rock-bound shores of New England until the dawn of their revolutionary triumph; then take their subsequent struggles with the Indians, the second time with the mother country, with Mexico, with treason and nullification, and close the chapter with the immense sacrifices made during the present war, and in some slight degree you may realize the cost of civil liberty. Its money value may be computed so far as the expenditure of rational currency is concerned, but where is the voice, or pen, that can describe the cost of so much precious blood and life '(Yet these are parts of liberty's price. Every drop of blood, every fallen brave, every tear, every throb of anguish, every broken household, every vacant chair, every lonely grave, is so much paid into the treasury of liberty. It demanded an Ellsworth, a Lyons, a Baker, a McPherson, a McCook, a Lytic, a Mitchell, and time would fail to mention a Patrick, an Elstner and Leek, of our own city, and a thousand others whose names have been rendered by her immortal.

We have met her demands as often as they came, until, at last, we thought her satisfied; and, radiant with sacrifice and victory, we went up to receive her blessings, rendered to her on the 14th instant our grateful homage, and returned prepared to enjoy the rich fruits that were in store for us. when again her voice was heard mingling with the dying throbs of treachery and treason — "one sacrifice more" ere my triumph is complete. "Who is it? It starts from every heart. Is it one of our gallant generals who have triumphantly led our armies to victory? No! Who then? No less a personage than the Captain of this ship that was at that moment furling her sails ready to enter the port of peace. Not One of the disciples, but the "Master." In order that the work may be well done, the Chief must die.

Here I would, if I could, drop the curtain over this last and grander sacrifice; but as the claims of God and Liberty must meet with full satisfaction, I say to them in this hour of grief: Here we are ready to lay upon thy glorious altar more of goodness — more of political worth — more of true virtue — more of mercy — more of charity and love than thou hast ever before received in one personal offering. O, Liberty! here tonight, on thy bloody but triumphant altar, we offer thee the Moses of the nineteenth century— the Winkelried of America — the Howard of the Union — the

"Wilberforce of over three millions of liberated slaves — the Luther of the world's future political status — the admired of earth — the idol of freemen everywhere—the loved of our hearts. Go search the world for living men, where will you find his like again! Will not this suffice? Is not his blood sufficient to put out the remaining fires of treason, and from its lofty eminence, will it not spread o'er all the land until it becomes the cementing bond of eternal fidelity to the Union? Grant it, O God of Liberty!

Denied the privilege of entering with us into the promised land, may his freed spirit, not many days hence, be sent, as a ministering angel, to guide us as we enter into the possession of the heritage given to us by this last and heaviest payment.

But I am to speak of the results that will, in all human probability, flow from the death of the President. Every death, to him who studies the providences of God, is intended for some good, greater or less. Moses was called to die just at a time when they were about to enter the Promised Land. God gave him the sight, but denied him an entrance. The reason assigned by the writer is, that Moses, at some time while leading the children of Israel, displeased God. {Here the speaker referred to the history of Moses.} But there were other reasons. The children of Israel were an idolatrous people. They had more than once merged the Creator in their worship of the creature. The history states that in the course of their journeyings and sufferings they murmured at Moses, disliked his administrations, yet on their near approach to deliverance, their murmurings were turned into affection, their complaints into rapturous praises, and they had already said, in their hearts, "great is Moses," instead of "great is the God of Moses." They, in their rejoicings, were ready to say, "See what Moses has done for us." They lost sight of the Author of their success, while looking upon the instrument. Here God saw that the work of Moses was complete, and taking him up into the mountain, he convinced him of the fact.

Again, Moses was a merciful man, and God may have said, in his heart, " ho has too often stayed my anger against this people; they must now pass into other hands, in order that mercy does not become a crime." May I not apply the above to our modern Moses? No man ever encountered as much difficulty in trying to administer the government of this country as Mr. Lincoln. Opposition, not only from its enemies, but its avowed friends, met him at every step. There were heard murmurs and objections to his administration; many expressed fears and doubts, yet as he at last brought the nation to the banks of deliverance, over thirty millions of freemen began to exclaim, Great is Abraham Lincoln! And in the spirit of sudden idolatry, that has ever characterized us as a nation, we were ready to sink the Author of our happiness and deliverance in the honored instrument. If not this, another reason is prominent. Our President was a man of unbounded mercy — never was as much mercy enshrined in humanity since the days of the Nazarene as was in him. He was devoid of all prejudice, of all personal resentment, of all feelings of hatred; in fact, mercy was more pre-eminent in his administration than justice, and, I dare not say tonight, that it was not right, yet, like Moses of old; his work was completed when mercy seemed to interfere with the claims of justice. I may be wrong in this remark, God forgive me if I am, yet I can but feel, riven by grief as I am, that when the dark shadows of treason, in the garb of an assassin, entered that box in the theatre of the capital, that mercy folded her snowy pinions and left treason to the thunderbolts of justice, to return no more until this last great wrong is wiped out in the death or expatriation of every leader of this foul rebellion. {Continued cheering.} The wrongs of liberty culminated in the assassination of Mr. Lincoln, and, minister as I am, I feel like saying tonight, that these wrongs must be avenged. One of the results of this execrable act is the opening of our eyes to the fact that in the midst of our joy we were about to take to our bosom a half frozen adder, only frozen by the power of our arms, to warm it into life again.

Yes, to make them great again, who sought their country's ruin."

Now, the adder must die! {Immense applause.} Hence I feel to say, an eye for an eye, a tooth for a tooth. For every drop of blood that flowed from the veins of this great and good man, at least one leading Rebel must die, or be banished from this country forever.

{The scene that followed this cannot be described. Hundreds rose to their feet; thousands of handkerchiefs waved all over the hall, and it was many seconds ere the eloquent preacher could proceed."}

By the unnumbered graves of our slain sons, husbands and brothers; by the wails of America's weeping Rachels; by all the sorrows of widowhood and orphanage: by all the graves of those who were starved to death in Rebel prisons; by the dark emblems of mourning that surround me this night; by the mercy that we have shown to our enemies; in their name, I demand that this climax of their terrible iniquity be wiped out at the bands of the sternest justice that this nation is capable of administering. (Continued cheering.) Not only is this duo to us, but due to the world at large. We must now set the seal to our triumphs in the death or banishment of those who, though fostered, educated and fed by the genius and liberality of our free institutions, willingly and knowingly raised their bloody hands (not only stained with the blood of their slaves, and with the precious blood of the republic, but the blood of one of the best men of modern times,) to strike down the best government of earth.

Another result, I trust, will consist in our valuing the blessings of liberty more, and a living consciousness of the great fact that while we propose God will dispose. Let us learn to lean more upon God than man. Let us cultivate and cherish more of those great principles of righteousness "that alone exalteth a nation." Let us reverence God more and man loss. Another great result of his death will he to cement more firmly our love to country; for, as said before, this love will and must be in proportion to its cost. And as we cannot compute this, let all nations say of us in time to come, that our love to the Union and the great principles of civil liberty cannot be estimated. But time and your patience forbids in dwelling longer on this dark picture. Mr. Lincoln the pure, unselfish, unprejudiced patriot is at this hour in the land of perpetual freedom — the land where treason, assassination and their authors cannot go. His mighty work is done, and I hear a voice from that heavenly world saying, "Blessed are the dead who die in the Lord. Yea, saith the spirit, they rest from their labors, and their works do follow them." His works shall follow him; though dead, he shall still speak. Let us hearken to his voice. To the young men, who so largely compose this audience, I would say, listen to him. Imitate his glorious life. Live like him, for God, your country, and the rights of all men. Be pure in heart and purpose as was our great President. Be loyal as he was loyal. Love all men — whether white or black, bond or free — as he loved them. Be merciful as he was merciful. Let the inspiration of his memory be one of the guiding stars of your future life. As a citizen of our Republic he was true to his citizenship. As a patriot he has no superior. Love of liberty and country was with him a principle — a living, vitalizing, active principle to which home, friends, party, and all else were subordinate. He suffered no desire for ease, or pleasure, or the honors of the world to swerve him from the path of duty, and he only died that the triumph of liberty, and your future happiness, might be complete. He died to perpetuate through all time the blessings that must flow from a government like ours. He died in order "that the heel of the old flag staff might forever crush the rattlesnake's head." Yea, that the many-headed monster of treason should be buried beneath the ear of genuine republicanism, beyond the hope of our future resurrection. He died amid the ringing of fetters as they fell from the enslaved millions of the South; as the cruel crack of the overseer's lash fell for the last time upon the back of the last slave of America. My fellow-citizens, to die thus is to die triumphantly.

> For whether on the gallows high,
> Or by the assassin's hand;
> The fittest place for man to die,
> Is when he dies for man!"

Such a death is to be envied; for he who dies for the freedom of man never dies. Nay, "the earth may pass like a wild dream away, the very heavens be rolled together as a scroll, but He, beneath whose feet the sun and stars are but dust," has said, "that the memory of such as Lincoln shall never die." Such memories shall live; they shall never grow dim with age. They are graven upon the very mountains, and in the valleys of the land they loved so well. And in the time to come, from the foam-crested waves of the Atlantic to those of the wild Pacific, as they sing lullabys of freedom to the setting sun; from the circling lakes, the guardians of liberty on the north, to the dark waters of the gulf, across which to night our victorious banner flashes defiantly at the enemies of republican government, their names shall be chanted in notes of gladness and songs of grateful remembrance, and the youths of other days shall come from afar to visit their graves, while the freed nations of earth shall make their way across thousands of liberty's triumphant battlefields, across freed continents and empires, to pay their grateful homage at the shrine of the glorious superstructure of Liberty, erected on this continent by the lives, suffering, and death of such as Abraham Lincoln, twice President of these United States.

Once again, and I am done. As was said this morning, so we repeat again, "the United States dies not with Mr. Lincoln; "on the other hand, I cannot but believe that his death gives it a newer and better existence. Let us, then, his survivors, be true to the great principles for which he offered up his life. His mantle has fallen upon a worthy man. In President Johnson I recognize many qualities of his predecessor. Like him, he is from the people, and knows how to sympathize with them. His past record shows him to be a true patriot, a tried lover of the Union; and leaning upon God, with our prayers and unflinching support, he may, and I have no doubt will, prove to be the Joshua of our hopes, Despair not; the nation still lives, and its very existence calls us to work, for there is much to do. Our victories have not been common ones. The world never witnessed any more fierce or terrible, and as glorious in their results. We hesitated a long time before unsheathing the sword. At least until forbearance with southern Rebels and latterly assassins ceased to be a virtue. Then, and not till then, were northern swords unsheathed "The pine was then brought against the palm; "and tonight, after four years of bloody war, we begin to see the end — an end not ultimating in the extension "of the sum of all villainies," but an end that looks upon the black monster, cradled in its dying couch, and by its side, already dead, is that other horrible thing Secession.

Yes, four years ago, on Friday last, Charleston was drunk with whisky and joy over the fall of Sumpter. Already in their wild imaginings the new government, conceived in gross iniquity and wrought upon to great wrongs, slavery and secession was established, and the land of the despised Yankee was soon to fall an easy prey to southern chivalry! Alas! For the fatuity of human expectations, especially when founded in wrong.

The glory of Charleston has passed away, and only a few hours ago, the very man upon whom the Charlestonians loved to heap their maledictions, (Beecher) re dedicated Sumpter and Charleston to God, and the rights of all men. We accepted of war, and firm in our convictions of right; strong in our determination to conquer, putting our trust in God, we went forth to conquer. Our trust in Him was not misplaced.

" For who that loans on his right arm was ever yet forsaken! What righteous cause can suffer harm if He its part has taken? Though wild and loud and dark the cloud, — Behind its folds His hand upholds The calm sky of tomorrow."

That tomorrow has at last come, and though its bright light is somewhat dimmed by our grief, yet it is the glorious harbinger of an honorable peace. The past four years have been fraught with much of sadness and sorrow, but ere four more pass, I have faith to believe, that the sun will again shine upon these States united and happy. Ere that time, if faithful to our high interests, every sword on this vast continent will have been forever sheathed for want of some opponent to liberty to subdue. As before said, there is much for us to do. War's desolations must be repaired; southern loveliness must be restored; ruined plantations redeemed from decay; ash piles turned again into habitations for freemen to live in. Over the fields now enriched by the best blood of earth must come again the white cotton, made more lovely and productive than ever, because planted and tilled by the hands of free labor. The poor whites must be raised by education and social influence to their true position in society; and last, but not least, the Negro must be educated and taught to value the blessings of freedom. Churches that have only rung to the groans and sufferings of the dying, must ring again to the songs of Zion, and the voice of God's ministers. Schoolhouses, so long vacant, must be reoccupied with southern children, and, if necessary, in order to a greater love for the Union, with Yankee teachers and Yankee books. Soldiers' homes are to be built, soldiers' widows to be provided for, soldiers' orphans to be educated, and, rising above all this, our country must be watched over with a zealous eye. A higher state of morals must pervade our political parties — enter into our legislative halls— possess the minds of our legislators, and all that pertains to religious and civil liberty, sacredly cared for. [Renewed applause.] Other thoughts crowd in upon me but I forbear. Peace is not yet declared, but it must soon come; I think without another battle — without the shedding of any more blood, save those who must expiate their guilt, and die as a warning to traitors and assassins in all the time to come. Our tribute of respect over, let us retire from this beautiful temple loving God and our country more. Mourning the loss of liberty's chieftain, let us keep his bright example over before us and go on in the glorious work of re-establishing this Union upon a rock more lasting than time, on principles that are almost as immutable as God himself. Then, when our race, like his, is run, nothing can give us more pleasure, save the presence of Jesus, than that of seeing the flag for which our President died waving over us, with not only its present number of stars, but many more added, all resplendent with freedom's light, telling us, in our dying moments, that America was always liberty's cradle, but never its grave.

Rev. John Falkner Blake
April 16, 1865

A SERMON

ON THE

Services and Death of Abraham Lincoln,

PREACHED IN

CHRIST CHURCH, BRIDGEPORT, CONN.,

EASTER SUNDAY, APRIL 16th, 1865.

REPEATED IN THE

NORTH CONGREGATIONAL CHURCH, BRIDGEPORT,

APRIL 19th, 1865.

BY

REV. JOHN FALKNER BLAKE,

RECTOR OF CHRIST CHURCH, BRIDGEPORT.

SERMON.
DEUT. iii: 23, 24, 25.

And I besought the Lord at that time, saying,

O Lord God, thou hast begun to shew thy servant thy greatness, and thy mighty hand: for what God is there in heaven or in earth that can do according to thy works, and according to thy might?

I pray thee, let me go over, and see the good land that is beyond Jordan, that goodly mountain, and Lebanon.

DEUT. xxiv: 1-6.

And Moses went up from the plains of Moab unto the mountain of Nebo, to the top of Pisgah, that is over against Jericho: and the Lord shewed him all the land of Gilead, unto Dan,

And all Naphtali, and the land of Ephraim, and Manasseh, and all the land of Judah, unto the utmost sea,

And the south, and the plain of the valley of Jericho, the city of palm trees, unto Zoar.

And the Lord said unto him, This is the land which I swore unto Abraham, unto Isaac, and unto

Jacob, saying, I will give it unto thy seed: I have caused thee to see it with thine eyes, but thou shalt not go over thither.

So Moses the servant of the Lord died there in the land of Moab, according to the word of the Lord.

Our Church has appointed this season for the celebration of one of the great Festivals of the Christian year. We are accustomed at Easter to come to the house of God, and, while our souls are overflowing with Joy--to mingle our glad voices in triumphant songs, and to cry out from the depths of grateful hearts, "The Lord is risen." But, this year, a greater than the Church --Almighty God-- has appointed the day as a day of trouble and anguish, and again is brought to pass throughout the land, that which was spoken by Jeremiah the prophet saying: "In Rama was there a voice heard, lamentation and weeping, and great mourning." It seems as if "there was not a house in which there was not one dead."

The people's shout of victory has not yet ceased echoing from hill to hill; but it is drowned in the wail of agony, which comes up from a broken-hearted nation. On Good Friday, God's great deliverance was so fresh in our thoughts, that we scarcely knew how to fast and mourn; but on this Easter, His hand is so heavy upon us, that we are constrained to hang our harps upon the willows and sit down and weep; for we know not how to sing!

The leader and liberator of the American people has fallen by the dastardly hand of an assassin, whose accomplice, another cowardly adherent of the foulest cause ever known under Heaven, has, with bloody hand, forced his way to the sick-bed of our chief Minister of State--lying already near to the gate of Death--and attempted to plunge a dagger into his heart!

Our beloved President is dead! Lost forevermore to us! Lost forevermore to his country! What is there so dear, that you would not freely have given it to have saved him for the nation? I know that there are thousands of patriots, the language of whose hearts today is, "Would to God I had died for thee!" I am sure there are those here present, who, if the Almighty God had given them the choice, would have said: "Take my child, my only child; but, oh God, spare the head of the nation."

I know the depth of your love for our murdered President, and therefore I ask you to weep with me today while we consider his late relations to us as a people. As I ponder over them, they seem to me to bear a striking analogy to those which Moses sustained to the children of Israel.

First, if we ask how Mr. Lincoln came to be the President of the United States, I think the spontaneous answer of every heart will be, God called him to the position, even as He called Moses.

When we consider the position of the young Hebrew in the household of Pharoah, it seems impossible that he could ever become the liberator of the Hebrew slaves. From infancy he had been brought up in the palace. All its glories were around him to dazzle, all its luxuries at his command to enervate him. He was so high in the favor of the royal family, that he was called "the son of Pharoah's daughter," and there was even reason to believe that he might one day sit upon Pharoah's throne. On the other hand there were the despised children of Abraham, slaves of the king, oppressed by cruel taskmasters. Who would have supposed that, from out the palace of the oppressor, he would come forth who was to bid the oppressed go free? that Moses, spurning the pomp of Pharoah's court, would himself be their leader? Yet so it was; for God said: "So let it be."

It was equally improbable to human reason, that Abraham Lincoln should be the President of the United States. Born, and brought up, in the land of slavery, in the State of Kentucky, accustomed to the manual labor of the farm and of the forest, associating with unrefined and uneducated people, until he shared somewhat in their characteristics, but thirsting for knowledge, and rising superior to circumstances, we find him after many years established as a humble lawyer in the State of Illinois.

It was here that the nation found him. Why did it seek him? Not for his fame, for he was comparatively unknown outside of his own State. Not for the greatness of his intellect, for that had not then been made manifest. Not for his unequalled honesty, for such a quality was hardly to be expected in a Western lawyer. The politician may say he was sought because he was available. The Christian, as he regards subsequent events, will say, "GOD raised him up to be the President of the United States." The man came with the age, and God sent them both.

As we regard the difficulties which stood in the way of Moses, on entering upon the work that he was called to perform, we wonder that he was not appalled. The power seemed to be all on one side. What could the unarmed slaves do in a contest with the armed hosts of Egypt? But Moses remembered that God was on his side, and he became lion-hearted.

When our people had spoken through the ballot box, and decided who should be their President, who can measure the difficulties and dangers which beset the man of their choice? You remember how the flag had just been dishonored, and that the then President sat in his chair "like a sleeping Jove,"--the thunderbolts which God and his country had given him to hurl, with giant force, at the foes of the nation, lying idle and harmless in his hand. You remember how he was surrounded by corrupt cabinet officers--may their names go down to history eternally infamous; for they had been cooperating with the enemies of the country to deliver it up to them. You remember how the ships of war had been sent to peaceful foreign ports; how the public monies had been squandered--how the munitions of war had been placed in the hands of the foe. You remember how the constitutionally elected President of the country had to creep to his post of danger at the Capitol in disguise--how it required all the skill of the Lieutenant-General to prevent the rising of a mob on the day of Inauguration-how soldiers had to be mingled with the crowd who witnessed the ceremony, with strict injunctions to each, to watch every person near him, lest a deadly weapon should be aimed at the President elect while he was taking the oath of office. I was in that crowd, and I well remember the intense anxiety, which was felt. I recall too that the Lieutenant General sank exhausted on his chair in the evening, saying: "Thank God the day has passed without bloodshed! It is more than I expected!" You remember how nearly half the States were in rebellion, and that we expected daily to hear of the assassination of the new President; and as you ponder upon these and other difficulties and dangers, do not the circumstances in which our lamented President first took charge of affairs seem appalling? It was the Lord's work, which was to be done; His servant began its performance without fear, and he was saved, for God's hand was over him, until it was all finished.

What was the work, which Moses was called to do? It was nothing less than to deliver his race from slavery. The work before our late beloved President was the same. God called him to free the nation. When we formed what we called a free country, and declared to the world that "to all men inalienably belong life, liberty, and the pursuit of happiness," African slavery--shame on us--was allowed to remain in many of the States. We proclaimed the truth with our lips, and denounced it as a lie by our actions. We sowed to the wind, and we reaped the whirlwind.

We became a nation of slaves. The slaveholders became slaves to the worst of passions. They gradually went backward, till they arrived at a state of semi-barbarism. We want no better proof of this than the commencement of this war, which, in the words of one of the ablest of the traitors-- and I quote them because they cannot be too deeply impressed upon our minds--"was inaugurated not because the Government was unrighteous; not because the Southern States had not received fair and honorable treatment; not because they had not enjoyed more than their share of privilege and office, but for the purpose of establishing a government, in the nineteenth century, whose corner stone should be human slavery;" an institution which England--with all her selfishness--had abolished in her colonies, while even Russia had overthrown--as unworthy of the age--a system far superior to American slavery. If this is not proof sufficient, then take as evidence the Southern conduct of the war. Let their cruelties--which would disgrace the wild tribes of Africa--speak; let the graves of the sixty thousand soldiers whom they murdered by starvation bear their testimony; and if this is not enough, ask yourself if any one, not possessed of the devil of slavery, could have murdered the South's best friend, or have attempted to assassinate a sick man in his bed.

But more than this; we of the free North became slaves to the slaveholders. We kneeled and knuckled to them. We gave up one right after another. We allowed our free New England hills to become their hunting grounds for panting fugitives. We gave up our liberty of speech and press. We proclaimed our ministers of Christ politicians, if they dared to pronounce the sacred obligations of a black man's marriage, or the right of a black woman to her own child, or the right of black people to the education of the minds which God had given them. Thus, then, black and white, we had all become slaves, and as God sent Moses to deliver the children of Israel from slavery, so, I believe, he sent Abraham Lincoln to deliver us.

We are not yet quite free. I do not know but some, today, will call me politician for defending the poor and lowly, and denouncing their oppression. If this is their definition of politicians, then I gladly accept the name, for they could call me by none of which I would be so proud. If this is to be a politician, I have always been one, and, God helping me, I shall always be one. We are not yet quite free, but our chains have become loose, and are about to fall from us. Soon we shall stand before the world as free men.

Go back again to the land of Egypt, and behold Moses making his appeals before Pharaoh. His words, at first, are without threats. He humbly, yet fearlessly, in the name of his God, prays for that which is due his oppressed people. When his appeals are not heeded, he thunders in the ear of the proud king the threatened judgments of the Almighty, and, when appeals and threats fail, the judgments come; disaster follows disaster, till the whole land groans, and at last "there is not a house in which there is not one dead."

Even so it was with our late leader. How earnest, how tender were his appeals to our misguided Southern brethren! How he tried to convince them by argument! How he appealed to every high and noble feeling! His first Inaugural address closed with the following words:

> "In your hands, my dissatisfied fellow-countrymen, and not in mine, is the momentous issue of civil war. The Government will not assail you.
>
> "You can have no conflict without being yourselves the aggressors. You have no oath registered in heaven to destroy the government; while I shall have the most solemn one to 'preserve, protect, and defend it.'

"I am loath to close. We are not enemies, but friends. We must not be enemies. Though passion may have strained, it must not break, our bonds of affection.

"The mystic cords of memory, stretching from every battle-field and patriot-grave to every living heart and hearthstone all over this broad land, will yet swell the chorus of the Union, when again touched, as surely they will be, by the better angels of our nature."

Thus he held out the olive-branch--thus he forbore threatening--but, when every gentle means failed, he proved to them that the magistrate "beareth not the sword in vain." The door of the temple of Janus was opened, and red and bloody war stalked through their land. The war-horse neighed and pranced upon the summits of all their hills. The tread of innumerable soldiers shook the earth as they marched over it--conquering and to conquer, capturing men, subduing cities, blasting and desolating the fertile fields. The ships of war thundered at the gates of all their ports, battered down their forts, and took possession of their harbors, till they fled like sheep from the whole coast. Again were they driven and scattered by our forces upon the land, and it was but as yesterday that the flower of their army surrendered; and now, powerless and stricken, the Southern confederacy is cursed of God and forsaken by

man. It stance before the world shivered and blasted like a forest struck by lightning. No bird sings in it--no leaf flutters on its scorched and blackened branches--yet, from out the ashes and desolation and darkness of that place of death and hell, creeps forth the solitary assassin, and, led on by the foul Fiend, strikes a blow which makes the heart of that nation to bleed whose sceptre it has in vain defied. Worthy conclusion of an infernal cause, which gives to law and liberty a martyr, and to itself eternal infamy. Amen and amen.
Not the Egyptians alone had Moses to contend with. He had scarcely passed from sight of the oppressor, when his own people began to murmur against their deliverer. They sighed for the fleshpots of slavery, and longed to return to bondage.

Here, again, how strong is the parallel! Was ever man murmured against, as was our late President? Friends and foes have alike cried out against him. Some denouncing him because he was too lenient--others because he was too severe--while still others have applied to him every vile and low epithet, which bad hearts could invent. How often has he had occasion to cry out: "Save me from my friends!" Yet in the midst of it all he went forward; "his eyes looked right on and his eyelids straight before him." He had but one aim. As Moses only thought of bringing his people to the Promised Land, so he had no thought but to save his country and to lead it to a glorious and united future. On his first journey to Washington he said in an address to the Mayor of the city of New York:

> "There is nothing that could ever bring me to willingly consent to the destruction of this Union, under which not only the great commercial city of New York, but this whole country, acquired its greatness, except it be the purpose for which the Union itself was formed. I understand the ship to be made for the carrying and the preservation of the cargo; and, so long as the ship can be saved with the cargo, it should never be abandoned, unless it fails the possibility of its preservation and shall cease to exist, except at the risk of throwing overboard both freight and passengers. So long, then, as it is possible that the prosperity and the liberties of the people be preserved in this Union, it shall be my purpose, at all times, to use all my powers to aid in its perpetuation."

In his first inaugural address he said:

> "I therefore consider that, in view of the Constitution and the laws, the Union is unbroken; and, to the extent of my ability, I shall take care, as the Constitution expressly enjoins upon me, that the laws of the Union shall be faithfully executed in all the States. Doing this, which I deem to be a simple duty on my part I shall perfectly perform it, so far as is practicable, unless my rightful masters, the American people, shall withhold the

requisition, or in some authoritative manner, direct the contrary.

"I trust that this will not be regarded as a menace, but only as the declared purpose of the Union, that it will constitutionally defend and maintain itself.

"In doing this, there need be no bloodshed or violence; and there shall be none, unless it is forced upon the national authority.

"The power confided to me will be used to hold, occupy, and possess the property and places belonging to the Government, and collect duties and imposts; but, beyond what may be necessary for these objects, there will be no invasion, no using of force against or among the people anywhere."

An eminent author said of him:

"Surrounded by all sorts of conflicting claims, by traitors, by half-hearted, timid men, by Border-State men and Free-State men, by radical abolitionists and conservatives, he has listened to all, weighed the words of all; waited, observed; yielded now here, and now there; but in the main kept one inflexible, honest purpose, and drawn the national ship through."

From the time he took his first oath of office till he went to his rest, his every official act was performed to this end. If other questions came up, and among them the slavery of the black race, the Almighty, and not man, forced them into the struggle. To use his own words: "I desire to save the Union--that must be preserved; and if it cannot be preserved with slavery, then slavery must cease." God ordered that the country could not be saved with slavery, and, glory to His name, slavery dies.

His interest in the soldiers, who stood sword in hand to help him to save the Union, was most profound. He delighted to be personally present on occasions when efforts were made to add to the comforts of the men suffering on the field. At a ladies' fair, when asked to give a word of encouragement, he remarked:

> "Ladies and gentlemen, I appear to say but a word. This extraordinary war in which we are engaged falls heavily upon all classes of people, but the most heavily upon the soldier. For it has been said, 'All that a man hath will he give for his life;' and, while all contribute of their substance, the soldier puts his life at stake, and often yields it up in his country's cause. The highest merit, then, is due to the soldier.
>
> "In this extraordinary war, extraordinary developments have manifested themselves,

such as have not been seen in former wars; and, among these manifestations, nothing has been more remarkable than these fairs for the relief of suffering soldiers and their families. And the chief agents in these fairs are the women of America.

"I am not accustomed to the use of language of eulogy; I have never studied the art of paying compliments to women: but I must say, that, if all that has been said by orators and poets since the creation of the world in praise of women were applied to the women of America, it would not do them justice for their conduct during the war. I will close by saying, God bless the women of America!"

That blessing was implored on every noble woman here, who in the silence of her own chamber has prayed and toiled for the brave children of the nation, and all the people say, Amen!

I cannot forbear here to say one word in regard to his personal interest in the lowly. An incident will illustrate what I mean. A newspaper correspondent, writing from Washington, says:

"I dropped in upon Mr. Lincoln on Monday last, and found him busily engaged in counting greenbacks. 'This, sir,' said he, 'is something out of my usual line; but a President of the United States has a multiplicity of duties not specified in the

Constitution, or acts of Congress: this is one of them. This money belongs to a poor negro, who is a porter in one of the departments (the treasury), and who is at present very sick with the small-pox. He is now in the hospital, and could not draw his pay, because he could not sign his name.

"I have been at considerable trouble to overcome the difficulty, and get it for him; and have at length succeeded in cutting red tape, as you newspaper-men say. I am now dividing the money, and putting by a portion labeled in an envelope with my own hands, according to his wish;' and his excellency proceeded to indorse the package very carefully. No one who witnessed the transaction could fail to appreciate the goodness of heart which would prompt a man, who is borne down by the weight of cares unparalleled in the world's history, to turn aside for a time from them to succor one of the humblest of his fellow-creatures in sickness and sorrow."

But to return. Moses leaned upon his God. Here was his strength. Without this he could not have performed the work, which God gave him to do. See him at the Red Sea. The people are murmuring--the waves are rolling before him--the hosts of the Egyptians are darkening behind him. With strong faith he looks up to Heaven and cries out to his God, and, lo! The answer comes, for "the

Lord said unto Moses, wherefore criest thou unto me? speak unto the children of Israel, that they go forward." Moses in faith lifts his rod, the waters open, and stand on either side as a wall, and the children of Israel pass through dry shod; but the hosts of Pharoah, following, are engulfed in the deep.

And now it is with grateful joy that I turn to our late President's trust in his God. Do you remember that, when he left Springfield for Washington, he asked the people of that town to pray for him? He said to them:

> "My friends, no one can appreciate the sadness I feel at this parting. To this people I owe all that I am. Here I have lived more than a quarter of a century. Here my children were born, and here one of them lies buried. I know not how soon I shall see you again. A duty devolves upon me which is perhaps greater than that which has devolved upon any other man since the days of Washington. He never would have succeeded, except for the aid of Divine Providence, upon which he at all times relied. I feel that I cannot succeed without the same divine aid which sustained him; and in the same Almighty Being I place my reliance for support; and I hope that you, my friends, will all pray that I may receive that divine assistance, without which I cannot succeed, but with which success is certain. Again I bid you all an affectionate farewell."

I am sure they granted his request. Who has not prayed for him? How fervently have your prayers always gone up from this house, and from your private closets, that God would help him! Glory be to His name, our prayers were answered, and God did help him!

To the President of the Ohio Senate he said:

> "It is true, as has been said by the President of the Senate, that very great responsibility rests upon me in the position to which the votes of the American people have called me. I am deeply sensible of that weighty responsibility. I cannot but know, what you all know, that without a name, perhaps without a reason why I should have a name, there has fallen upon me a task such as did not rest upon the "Father of his Country;" and, so feeling, I cannot but turn, then, and look to the American people, and to that God who has never forsaken them."

To the Synod of the Old School Presbyterians of Baltimore, who waited upon him in a body, he said:

> "I saw, upon taking my position here, I was going to have an administration, if an administration at all, of extraordinary difficulty.

"It was, without exception, a time of the greatest difficulty this country ever saw. I was early brought to a lively reflection that nothing in my power whatever, or others, to rely upon, would succeed, without direct assistance of the Almighty. I have often wished that I was a more devout men than I am: nevertheless, amid the greatest difficulties of my administration, when I could not see any other resort, I would place my whole reliance in God, knowing all would go well, and that he would decide for the right.

"I thank you, gentlemen, in the name of the religious bodies which you represent, and in the name of our common Father, for this expression of respect. I cannot say more."

You are most of you familiar with the following incident. A gentleman, having recently visited Washington on business with the President, was, on leaving home, requested by a friend to ask Mr. Lincoln whether he loved Jesus. The business being completed the question was kindly asked. The President buried his face in his handkerchief, turned away and wept. He then turned and said: "When I left home to take this chair of State I requested my countrymen to pray for me; I was not then a Christian. When my son died, the severest trial of my life, I was not then a Christian. But when I went to Gettysburg, and looked upon the graves of our dead heroes, who had fallen in defense of their country, I then and there consecrated myself to Christ. Yes, indeed, I do love Jesus."

How have his proclamations and speeches been full of childlike devotion to his Heavenly Father? Was ever such a document sent forth by the head of any nation as his last inaugural address? It could not have come forth but from the depths of a Christian heart.

The President was a man of prayer. An incident has gone the rounds of the newspapers, which illustrates this. As related in the public prints, it has many inaccuracies. It was given to me two or three days after it occurred, by an eminent clergyman of the city of New York. A distinguished lawyer of New York, himself a professing Christian, and an intimate friend of my informant, had occasion some time since to see the President in Washington. He went to his house, met Mr. Lincoln, and asked for an interview of one hour. Mr. Lincoln said that the press of public duties forced him to decline such an interview. He urged that it was important. The President still declined. The gentleman was leaving when Mr. Lincoln stopped him and asked if he would be willing to come at five o'clock the next morning. He gladly agreed to do so, and arrived at the house next morning, as he supposed, at five o'clock. On consulting his watch by the street lamp, he found he had made a mistake of an hour, and that it was only four o'clock. He determined to walk about the grounds until the time agreed upon. Coming near a window of one of the rooms of the presidential mansion, he heard sounds of apparent distress. On listening, he found it was the voice of the President, who was engaged in an agony of prayer. The burden of his petition was: "Oh God! I cannot see my way; give me light. I am ignorant, give me wisdom; teach me what to do and help me to do it. Our country is in peril. Oh God! it is Thy country; save it for Christ's sake!" Here the gentleman felt his position to be questionable, and passing on he left the President with his God. On entering the house he mentioned what he had heard to the usher, who informed him that the President spent the hour between four and five every morning in prayer.

Here, I think, was the secret of his single, straightforward course. He has cried to God, and God has told him to go forward, sometimes when difficulties have been before and behind him as great as those which beset Moses; but he has gone forward in the strength of God, and deeper waters than those of the Red Sea have been opened for him, and mightier foes than the Egyptians have been overwhelmed behind him.

Moses, at last, comes to the borders of the Promised Land. He has shared the weary toils and marches of his people, and with them has arrived almost at the land of Canaan. For a long time they linger on the border, and then the Lord commands him to go up to the top of Mount Pisgah, that he may behold the Promised Land. "And Moses went up from the plains of Moab unto the mountain of Nebo, to the top of Pisgah, that is over against Jericho: and the Lord showed him all the land of Gilead unto Dan, and all Naphtali, and the land of Ephraim, and Manasseh, and all the land of Judah unto the utmost sea, and the South, and the plain of the valley of Jericho, the city of palm trees, unto Zoar. And the Lord said unto him, this is the land which I swore unto Abraham, unto Isaac, and unto Jacob, saying: I will give it unto thy seed. I have caused thee to see it with thine eyes, but thou shalt not go over thither. So Moses the servant of the Lord died there in the land of Moab, according to the word of the Lord." Some time before, Moses had prayed that he might enter the Promised Land, but God refused his prayer.

How affecting--how beautiful is the parallel here! For more than four long years our late beloved President has borne this nation upon his heart. He has shared her troubles--yea, he has carried more of her sorrows than any of her children. Sorrowfully, wearily, prayerfully, he has watched and waited for the dawn of peace. We have long believed that we have been near to the glad morning of peace. Victory after victory has come to us. For many a day every flash from the electric wire has brought us good tidings from Tennessee, from Alabama, from Georgia, from South Carolina, from North Carolina--now the capture of Atlanta--now the triumphant march through Georgia--now the fall of Savannah--now of Wilmington--now of Charleston--now the victorious raids of Sheridan--and now the cries of despair from the traitors' capital Could the end be far off? How easily can we imagine the President kneeling in that room in the nation's house, offering to the God of nations the prayer of Moses: "Oh Lord God, Thou hast begun to show thy servant thy greatness, and thy mighty hand; for what God is there in heaven or in earth that can do according to thy works and according to thy might; I pray Thee, let me go over, and see the good land that is beyond Jordan, that goodly mountain and Lebanon." How he must have longed and prayed to see the blessed result of God's work, of which he had been the instrument! And, had his prayer been granted, I believe he would have been ready to say with Simeon: "Lord, now lettest Thou thy servant depart in peace, for mine eyes have seen thy salvation."

Last Sunday, the last he was to spend upon earth, came the news of the surrender of Lee's great army, which, as we believe, was the deathblow of the rebellion. God spared him to see this. The plot was prepared to take his life on the fourth of March, but God spared him to see this. Blessed be His holy name. It is as if in mercy he took him up the mountain, to show him the good things which he had prepared for his nation; but, as Moses was not permitted to enter the promised land with his people, so he was not permitted to partake with us of the blessings which he has so laboriously earned for us, and for which we shall all love him and weep for him till we are cold in death.

But let us not sorrow as those without hope. The

land of Canaan was a goodly land; it flowed with milk and honey. Sweet would have been its rest to Moses after his weary marches in the wilderness; but God had prepared for him a fairer land than that of Canaan, a more glorious mountain than that of Lebanon--the Canaan beyond the flood--the everlasting hills.

And so of our revered President--the liberator of his people--our beloved friend. It would have been a bright, a glorious day for him, could be have seen the nation which he had saved once more united and happy--purified as by fire and rejoicing in the blessing of God. But his Father and ours has taken him to a better land than this. Having finished his work--a work that will live forever --we believe he has entered into his rest. And though

> "The mourners throng the way, and from the steeple
> The funeral-bell tolls slow;
> Yet on the golden streets the holy people
> Are passing to and fro;
>
> "And singing as they meet: '
> Rejoice! Another Long waited for, is come;'
> The Saviour's heart is glad, a younger brother
> Hath reached the Father's home!"

Even his enemies are willing now to acknowledge his worth. I am credibly informed that yesterday, when the rebel General Ewell heard of the assassination, he wept like a child.

And now farewell, beloved President! The nation, without distinction of party or sect, mourns for thee as a stricken family. A liberated people says to thee: "Well done, good and faithful servant," and our Father says to thee: "Enter thou into the joy of thy Lord."

Comforting a Nation

Rev. A. D. Mayo
April 16, 1865

THE NATION'S SACRIFICE.

ABRAHAM LINCOLN.

TWO DISCOURSES,

Delivered on Sunday Morning, April 16, and Wednesday Morning, April 19, 1865,

IN THE

CHURCH OF THE REDEEMER,

CINCINNATI, OHIO.

By A. D. MAYO, Pastor.

THE NATION'S SACRIFICE.
"Without shedding of blood is no remission."
-HEB. ix, 22.

When God is speaking, who shall open his mouth! He speaks to us today, and his word is the old voice of inspiration: "Without shedding of blood is no remission."

All shedding of blood is by God's permission. Not one act of violence, not one destruction of life, not one drop of human blood shed, without his knowledge and consent. For God is infinite love, and in His perfect providence all things work together for good. Even the things that seem so terrible that men tremble as if there were a Prince of Darkness, and he were master of the universe, are compelled to do His sovereign will. He maketh the wrath of man to praise him, and the remainder of wrath shall He restrain.

Ever since the beginning of the world the friends of falsehood and sin have believed that the right could be put down by shedding the blood of the righteous. Cain believed he could destroy the true worship of God by slaying Abel, the servant of God. And since his day every wicked and foolish man, every great despot, every God-defying class, every desperate member of every party of unrighteousness the world has seen has been crazed by this stupendous delusion that the Truth and Justice and Holiness of God Almighty could be driven away from the earth by killing the friends of God and man.

So the world, for four thousand years, has been full of blood. None of it rests upon the hands of the consistent friends of God and man, for all they have shed has been in defense of everlasting righteousness. It all rests on the souls of the enemies of Truth and Goodness; for they never have overcome the hideous delusion that they could slay the Truth by slaughtering its defenders. Oh! What an Aceldema have they made of this fair earth by their insanity! How many of the wisest, best, and loveliest--the glory of all ages and all lands--have they sent to their God, through bloodstained paths! How many of the wicked, the worst of the earth, have they also sent to judgment in blood! How many, in all conditions of spiritual life, have they drowned in this bloody sea of wrath! But yet, the wrath of mail shall praise Him.

One would have thought that when the concentrated falsehood and injustice of the ancient time, wielding the power of the Roman Empire, nailed Jesus, Son of God and man, to the bloody cross, that the wrath of man had done its worst. And when, out of the shedding of Christ's blood came Salvation for even his own murderers, when the Roman power that slew him at last bent before his gentle sway, so that the very names of Rome and the cross are fixed together till the end of time--one might have hoped that wicked men would have learned the impotence of shedding blood to help the wrong. But wicked men do not learn such things. And every year since the sacrifice of Christ, the violent on earth have been peopling Heaven with martyrs and filling all lands with tears and blood.

And we have lived to behold what our eyes have seen during the last four years, reaching its climax of horrors in that strange deed which we can hardly yet believe has happened. We supposed, a few years ago, that the vast majority of mankind in civilized lands had finally learned that no great wrong could be upheld one hour by shedding of blood. But God has called us, in this new world, to behold what the peoples of the old world, the other side of the great waters, have witnessed so often--the awful delusion and wrath of that despotism which is the sum of all wrong against earth and Heaven. We did not believe what history had told us on her every bloody page, that a tyrant, or a class of tyrannical men would commit all crimes of which human nature is capable, under the vain fanatical belief that they could put man down and keep him down. So God has raised up, right among us, of our very hearts' kin, our friends, countrymen, associates, participators with us in all the blessed privileges of American life, a class of despots, who, within the last half century, have committed more crimes, and worse crimes, than any great aristocracy that yet has dominated in ancient or modern days. For I verily believe that when History comes to make out her awful record against the slave aristocracy of these United States of America, it will be seen that since it appeared as a consolidated social and civil power, half a century ago, it has done evil to a greater number of human beings, sinned against greater light, caused the death of more innocent men, affrighted this world with more ghastly and singular shapes of horror and wrath, and meanness, and cold cruelty, than any one set of wicked men has ever yet been able to achieve.

Oh, how blind we were, not to see that a class of men who deliberately began by the blasphemy of God in the systematic degradation of his image, man, to a brute, would do any vile or bloody thing which human nature could devise. Yet we did not see it for so many years. We said: no, these gentlemen and gentlewomen are our brothers and sisters, our associates in Church, in State, in society; they are dreadfully mistaken, and are now doing wrong to their bondmen, but they will hear the voice of our reason, our science, our religion; they will repent, and be reconciled, and at last do justice to their own enslaved, to us, to themselves, and to their country. And so we went on in our sin and blindness, strengthening their hands, arming them with new weapons of power, forgiving them faster than they could harm us. We might have known then they were inflicting the worst outrages ever conceived on three millions of their unhappy subjects; but we said: they are of another race, they are not quite men; and went on making them stronger and stronger to slay us.

And soon enough they began to shed the blood of our own proud race, and to do to us all the dreadful things they had done to our weaker brother. They began to insult and abuse, and murder our people who, among themselves, lifted up their voices against this great wrong of despotism. We loved the liberty of speech, and they began to kill men for speaking the truth about their sin; we loved the freedom of the press, and they destroyed the types, and assassinated the editors; we were more gentle and reverent in our treatment of woman than any people ever was, and they imprisoned women for teaching children to read the Bible; we were proud of our free labor, and they killed and drove away the emigrants to every Territory and State they had doomed to be their own; we favored free suffrage, but they tried to murder every man that voted for the freedom of all men; we supposed the pulpit would be a place of safety, but they hung and shot ministers of the Gospel of the Golden Rule, and set a price on Channing's head; we thought the scholar's gown a shield, but they drove away, with terrible threats, every scholar who would not prostitute his learning to the enslavement of mankind; we supposed the Senate was an ark of safety, but they came in and half slew the foremost of American scholars and philanthropists on the floor of the Senate.

Yet all this did not open our eyes. Then they tried their hand on a higher thing, and resolved to drown the nation herself in the blood of her freedom-loving citizens. Four years ago last Friday they opened war, and for four years they have waged a conflict that has not been so much a war as a Saturnalia of all crimes within the record of man. They knew that if they would destroy this great republic they must wade through oceans of blood, and do such deeds, accursed of God and man, as would astonish mankind; but they did not hold back.

Oh, what things they have done, my friends, during these years! They have caused to be slain in battle, or to be wounded, or to die of sickness, or to be prostrated by anxiety and excitement, and the terrible bewilderment of revolution, not less than a million human beings. They have caused to be destroyed enough property to educate every child on the globe into a Christian man or woman. They have killed men in every variety of ways. When the Union men and women and children of the South shall stand up in evidence against these enemies, no one of us will have the heart to read their story. They have redoubled their cruelty to their slaves, and forced them, at the bayonet's point, to work, yea, to fight, for their own enslavement. They have slaughtered women, murdered little children, butchered prisoners of war; they have deliberately starved to death thousands of white men taken captive in fair battle; they have insulted the remains of our slain. They mutilated the dead body of Dahlgren, and their best man, Robert Lee, sent to the father of the boy, as an excuse for the bloody deed, a pretended document of most barbaric import, said to have been found upon him, but deliberately forged and photographed, and then they hid his body for a whole year. They have enrolled bands of assassins, to steal upon border villages, five hundred miles from the seat of war, and shoot our citizens at mid-day. They have lighted up every ocean with the glare of our unarmed merchant ships. They have tried to burn our great cities, and involve thousands of every age and sex in wholesale destruction. Under the name of guerrilla operations, legalized by their sham government, they have disorganized human society itself over vast regions of our territory, and rendered life a daily peril and curse not fifty miles from our own doors. Sons murdering fathers, and brothers their brothers, and neighbors shedding one another's blood, even women betraying men to the assassin; all these things have become so common that we think of them as every day affairs.

But in spite of all this they did not prosper. Their cause waxed weaker as their wrath increased. The more freemen they killed the more men became freemen. They slaughtered our soldiers, but our ranks filled up and stood more firmly. They murdered Union men, but the Union grew, watered by their blood. They starved their prisoners, but our cause waxed full and mighty. Stung to very madness, they solemnly resolved at last that their black slaves should be made

soldiers, to gain their unholy ends; and before the ink was dry on that godless statute, their sham President and their sham Congress, their General-in-Chief and his powerful army, had disappeared by one blow of divine justice, so that they shall no more be known as a power on the earth, while the negro slave marched in, a conqueror and a freeman, under the Union, and occupied Richmond and Charleston, the Sodom and Gomorroh of their land of blood!
And then we thought the end of wrath had come. We said: these men must now see that there is no longer any hope in war, they know their despotism is dead forever; will they not come in and be our brethren once more? I have, during the last two weeks, travelled through seven free States, and in all their chief cities seen great crowds of people rejoicing over our victories, and the grandest thing I saw was the magnanimity of the people towards these, their mortal foes. Oh, if this Southern aristocracy, this prodigal son of the nation, this wanderer from the flock, would now come back to us, not in abject humiliation, but repentant, willing to be forgiven, willing to unite with us in building up the Republic, how gladly would this people, on its last great day of rejoicing, have gone out, like the Father, and taken the stricken one in to the great feast of love to God and man!

But no, it was not so to be. Wicked men upon earth always go on to the last result, and that result is to slay their truest friends, and quench their blind rage in the blood of the noblest who would die to save them.

There were two men in these United States, who were, under Providence, the most noted representatives of Human Liberty in all the land. The elder of the two was the greatest philosophic statesman that this or any republic has produced--a man whose vast mind beheld the regular onward march of Liberty from age to age, and who, in the midst of the apparent success of tyranny always perceived the coming deliverance of man. For forty years has this great and good man, gentle as a woman, genial as a little child, forgiving and kind and magnanimous to a fault, calmly uttered, in words that never purposely wounded a human being, or uttered one thought of private malignity or personal spite, the lofty prophecy, of the passing away of the despotism of the land. Accused of the worst motives and frailties, and intrigues, his real power has been in his wondrous glance over the field of our national life, so that like a watchman from a lofty tower, he has told off the passing hours of slavery, and called the people to welcome the morn of freedom. He never made a public mistake that was not the weakness of a heart too benevolent to credit what his reason told him was true of the enemies of man. He trusted so much in great ideas--he saw so clearly the inevitable conquest of the wrong by the right--that he was apparently careless what special measures should be enacted, or what special offenders put to shame. He once said to me: "We talk of vengeance upon the aristocracy of the South; let us only protect Liberty in the Union, and that aristocracy will at last come to us to be kept from starvation; and we, of the free States, will be obliged to nurse the South back to life like a sick child."

Among all the statesmen of the world, there was no man who, last Friday at sundown was at once so true a friend to the South, so true a friend to Union and Liberty, so firm a believer in the progress of man, so willing and eager to receive every repentant enemy of the Republic, and rejoice over his conversion, as WM. HENRY SEWARD, Secretary of State. He was born in the Empire State. He came on one side, of a Welsh ancestry, and for forty years of public life has been as inflexible in what he believed the cause of Freedom as the rocks and mountains, and noble people of that land. On the other side he was of Irish lineage, and no son of that afflicted race was ever more genial, more gracious, more winning, to friend and foe. And what American ever had a vision of the Union so lofty as his--a Union from which even her rebellious children should not always be cast out, which should lift up the lowliest to liberty, and teach the proudest monarchs on earth to rejoice in the prosperity of man?

And along with him I always saw his best-beloved son--a young man who seemed the perfect embodiment of his father's sweetness. He was so good, and simple-hearted and conscientious and gentle, that all men loved him as he walked the streets.

But there was one other in the land, greater than this statesman--because manhood is grander than genius, and silent and patient power nobler than the most gracious courtesy. ABRAHAM LINCOLN was the most faithful representative of the whole people, in public affairs, this world has yet seen. He came of a Northern Quaker paternity, and his maternity was out of the common people of old Virginia. He had worked through every kind of experience the people knew, up to the Presidency of the Republic. He was neither quick, nor brilliant, nor demonstrative; but his broad soul touched every class and race of our strangely mingled nationality. He felt in his blood what they were feeling and thinking; he knew what they could do, and bear, and achieve. He knew every kind of American men better than they knew themselves. He loved truth, and he loved man as well. Contemporaneously with Seward he saw and declared that the republic must be all free or all slave. Like Seward, he did not agitate for freedom so fiercely as some, for he saw its mighty coming afar off, and saved his strength to organize the new Republic. Apparently by the intrigues of policy, but really by the Providence of God, he was preferred to his great associate as candidate for President. The people knew by instinct whom they could trust, and chose him. He journeyed to Washington, so unpretending, so carefully, saying no harsh word; full of love for all the people of his vast domain. How he has carried the people through four years of frightful war, so that the republic is now triumphant, and slavery abolished, and the class that tried to destroy us going to its own place, history will say. And oh, how compassionate, how just, how like a father he has been to these mad children of the household. Has he said one word in bitterness of them? Has he pushed one measure in wrath? Has he knowingly done one deed that should prevent any rebellious man from coming to him as to a father? Read over again that last address of his--so broad, so practical, so wise, so magnanimous. Who ever went through such a four years so purely, so successfully, so lovingly, as he? As he awoke last Friday morning, he could have felt that his work was done; the army and navy of the Union everywhere triumphant; the people united in their rulers; slavery wounded to death; the nation ready to start anew on her glorious career of power and freedom. Had the deadliest rebel tyrant in all America so true a friend in the whole world that day as ABRAHAM LINCOLN?

So, here was the opportunity for this slave power to fill up the measure of its iniquity by striking at the life of the two men, of all others, who could have rescued it from its barbarity. And it did not hesitate a moment. Alas! The wretch who aimed at the father of his people did his work too well, and ABRAHAM LINCOLN has died, a blessed martyr, that his country might live! May God spare SEWARD to take one more observation of the political heavens and hells, and, in his own simple and majestic language, tell us what becomes of a power that signalizes its last occasion for repentance by the last crime of the assassination of the only men that could save it from perdition! May that blameless young man be spared to forgive the poor creature that tried to kill him because he would save his sick father's life!

And now what?

Nothing new. Only the same old thing that has been going on since the foundation of the world; all known to and approved by the Providence that never was beaten by any enemy of God or man.

One more martyr to Human Liberty. One more great and good man exalted by bloody death to the most sacred name in this new time. Is this a mistake of Providence? We have carelessly babbled that we could not choose a great man for President; the people did not know whom to trust. God has condescended to meet and dispose of that falsehood, once and forever. Never was ruler so instinctively recognized, so generously obeyed, so completely approved in his life as ABRAHAM LINCOLN by the Freemen of this Republic. And now that his great work is done, he has fitly put on the martyr's crown. WASHINGTON was Father of his County; our country owes to him her independent life. ABRAHAM LINCOLN was the Father of the American people: first under him was there one free people of the United States. Together in sainted memory will these men abide.

One more warning to the people of the nature of the power with which they contend. As long as there is a class in America that denies the humanity of man, it will do just what this slave aristocracy is now doing--what its leaders still advise it to do. It will argue till it is beaten--and then try to kill the priest, the scholar, the statesmen who have refuted it. It will fight as long as it can, with all the bravery and barbarity of savages, and when it surrenders as a warrior, reappear as an assassin. I do not say that all these rebel men and-women, that a majority of them, would personally have done this deed. But I say that a class that begins by denying humanity will end by doing all the infamy that was ever done, and then invent some new curse to scourge the world. This aristocracy has already committed all the crimes that men ever committed before; who shall say what hideous and strange enormity may startle us tomorrow? It will go on to its death as it has begun.

One more solemn announcement--that however merciful God and good men may be to individual sinners, yet for every wicked class and every unrighteous institution there is only eternal death. We may forgive every rebel in the Union of his special guilt, neither you, nor all men, nor God can forgive an aristocracy that has risen on hatred and contempt for man. This mighty revolution will go on, as every one like it has gone on, till that old slave aristocracy is ground to finer dust than now covers the grave of the man it slew. Last Friday it perhaps seemed that it might be saved, but we had only seen the beginning of the end. Before midnight it had opened between itself and modern times a gulf so deep and wide that no human arm can reach it more! It drove at the nation's heart four years ago, crying out: "Let us alone!" Well, now, at last, it is alone in God's world. It has put itself outside the pale of human fellowship, respect, and forgiveness. When the poor slave of that proud old caste flourished aloft his steel, and cried out, "Sic semper Tyrannis!" he spoke by the inspiration of God; he was the star actor of the great tragedy of modern days, for on that stage did the American slave aristocracy commit suicide, and pass away, forever more to be "let alone" by God and man. There did tyrannical old Virginia, having gone down through every phase of wickedness and meanness, perish, shouting her own motto and epitaph, and the world will never behold old Virginia any more.

Do you talk of vengeance! Look away across the abyss, to that Southern aristocracy, in its silent torment; look at poor old Virginia, and tell me what is left for you to do. We can live with LINCOLN away from the earth. But he was the last man that could have persuaded this American people to try to build anything good, out of that pile of rubbish--the slave aristocracy of the South. Henceforth the man who seriously proposes to resuscitate and reconstruct that old power may be permitted to go his way, as a maniac so hopeless that he can do no man harm. God seems to have said to us at the end of our rejoicings, last Friday night: -- All things are possible to your great energy, hope and love, save this one; see what this despotism will do on its way to everlasting perdition; henceforth waste no breath in calling to life what God has doomed to eternal death.

Who shall say the price is too great to pay for such a revelation from heaven? For now has come in the second era of this revolution. The great enemy is destroyed; we wounded him to death, and even while dying he clutched the pistol and through the head of our President, blew out his own foolish brains. Once for all, the American people understand which way lies hell. Every man not a fool can see today that one thing can never again be done. Next to knowing just what to do, it is good to know just what not to do. If ABRAHAM LINCOLN had lived he might have failed to show us just what to do in our new era of shaping the people's Republic. He has died to show us just what not to do in all the generations of man. What man, by his life and death, has decided a question so momentous before? God knows his own ways, and has used his servant, our Father, for the best.

Without the shedding of blood is no remission. Our blood has been poured out like water during four dreadful years, but all the time has God been lifting us thereby out of our sin. And now, that in our beloved President we all bleed today, we know all shall be saved to Freedom and Union, and all sins of the people be forgiven. We had said that LINCOLN must live till he became President of all the people--the loyal, who obeyed, and the disloyal, who defied the Republic through him. That was not to be. But now that he has passed through bloody death to his victory, he has gone up to his glorious inauguration in the heavens, as sovereign of the hearts of the whole American people. There he dwells, above the rage of his enemies and the folly of his friends; and there he will dwell in glory, till the children of all these wrathful and bloody men, one by one, shall be subdued by his mighty love, and come into the great Union of freedom. No one man could unite the American people today. But ABRAHAM LINCOLN is now a name about which all who inhabit this vast Republic shall gather in reverence while time endures. By the shedding of this sacred blood, our God and Saviour have told us there is remission for all the people's sins. Under the Saviour, Christ, shall this nation, through its chief of martyrs, be saved.

And now, Friends, Countrymen, Christians, what of us? Another true and tried man is President. Let every loyal soul rise up and stand today like a wall of strength by ANDREW JOHNSON, now, by the Providence of God, President of this Republic, regenerated and renewed by the sacrifice of bloody war.

By this event we are shown that no one man is great enough to do this mighty work before us, neither is any one man indispensable. Were every great man to fall to-morrow, there would still be left the American People, whose children and servants they are. We are that American People, God's chosen people of these modern days to lead the world to the freedom of all mankind. Every one of us must be somewhat nobler now that our great leader is gone. Let no breath now be wasted in barbaric curses, no power lost in indiscriminate vengeance. It would be childish in us to go off into a frenzy, or drift into disorder, or try to wash out his precious blood by spurning the corpse of the slave aristocracy! No! Let that abomination alone! Begin, to-morrow morning, to build up the American home, American industry, American religion, American society, the American Republic, in all its vast extent, with that decayed aristocracy left out and let alone. "Let alone" every man and woman that ties to that dead body. The new age is here. Have your doings, and sayings, and associations with living men and living things. Everywhere do better than you have yet done. Stop not to weep; but work and pray; and as you toil towards the new day the kindly face of our dear, dear father shall smile upon us with the same love that used to gleam out of those eyes, which assured us that when he did put off that great earthy body he would put on the spiritual body of a saint in heaven.

Oh, yes, look not down into that bloody grave, but upon these Easter flowers, today. Blessed types of that immortal beauty, which through all fleeting forms abides forever; let them teach us that all we love still lives; that all that is good and true lives; that God, and Christ, and martyrs, and "just men made perfect," live. Oh, yes, they live, all live who died that the Republic might endure. Little child, tender women, obscure soldier, unknown slave, heroic commander, priest, statesmen, President- all live more truly, more powerfully, more divinely, than they lived on earth. Can we be recreant with this cloud of witnesses looking on from the world of souls; with so many yet spared to earth who will gladly die that we may live; with God calling as he calls today? Oh, Thou who hast called Thy servant home, guide this people, and lead each one of us to his place in Thee.

"The righteous shall be in everlasting remembrance."--Ps. cxii, 6.

On the night of April 14,1865--the anniversary of the opening of the second American revolution, ABRAHAM LINCOLN, President of the United States, was slain by an assassin. Today, on the anniversary of the battle of Lexington, which opened the first American Revolution, also of the first bloodshed of the present war, in the streets of Baltimore, the loyal people of the United States observe his funeral solemnities.

It was a wise thought of the venerable Mr. HUNTER, Acting Secretary of State, to request the whole people of the Union to assemble at the hour of these funeral services, in their churches, for never has this people needed the lofty consolations of religion as on this day. Never before, in the history of the Republic has the attempt been made to involve the entire executive authorities of the nation in indiscriminate massacre. This astounding attempt, by permission of an inscrutable Providence, has partially succeeded; and at this solemn hour the Chief Magistrate is borne to the grave, while the Secretary and Assistant Secretary of State lie stricken, yet hovering on the borders of life and death. It is a momentous day in this people's history. Shall they, today, harden their hearts, breathe vows of eternal vengeance, and become, like their wrathful foes, a race of assassins and barbarians? Or shall this culmination of the crimes of a rebellious class only move them to a loftier love of liberty; a firmer resolution to extirpate human slavery; an inflexible determination to preserve and regenerate the Union; with the exercise of such a Christian spirit of mercy towards all repentant offenders as shall at once establish and adorn the majesty of the nation? Oh, may the ministers of God, who this day have the ear of the people, fail not to declare at once the Divine justice against our national sin, and the Divine compassion for all who repent of their complicity with it.

Last Sunday I counseled my people that this blow is the end of human slavery in this Republic, perhaps in the world; and that an aristocracy which had committed the last crime of assassinating its truest friends, can have no more hope of life in any world ruled by God. It is too early to say who among the individual criminals that have involved this Republic in war should suffer judicial punishment, or what that punishment shall be. When that question comes up it will be met and settled by the calm wisdom and conscience of the loyal American people. Today there can be nothing better done than to draw the portrait of the great and good man, who, on the very summit of triumph over his nation's foes, even while bending in a gracious attitude of mercy to a subdued enemy, became a martyr to Freedom. If we can hold in our souls a clear and full image of this noble American, we shall carry about with us a guide through all the perils to come. Let me, then, ask your attention to a discourse on the life and character of ABRAHAM LINCOLN.

ABRAHAM LINCOLN was born in Hardin County, Kentucky, February 12, 1809. His paternal ancestors were from Pennsylvania, of Quaker connection. They intermarried with Virginia women, and removed to Kentucky in 1782, where his grandfather was killed by the Indians, in 1784. Both his father and mother were born in Virginia. At seven years of age his family removed to Indiana, and little ABRAHAM, being then a large boy, was put to work with his axe to hew down the forests. For half a century he has plied that axe, till he has hewed his way up through the material, social, civil wilderness of our new American life, to the millennial day of Universal Liberty, guarded by Social Order and the People's Law.

For twelve years, till he was nineteen, he toiled in the forest, with only one year at school, and then went to New Orleans, as a hired hand on a flatboat. In 1830, at the age of twenty-one, he removed to Macon County, Illinois, and, true to his filial duty, helped build a log cabin for his father's family, and made rails enough to fence ten acres of land. Probably about this time he offered himself at the office of a lawyer now distinguished in Southern Indiana, as a student, but was rejected at once, as a hopeless subject. I doubt not God had better business for him just then, than learning Southern Indiana law. He was kept, like Washington, where he could learn of men, study the new life of the mighty West, and slowly matures into a noble growth of manhood. At twenty-two he helped build a boat, at twelve dollars a month, and then took it to New Orleans. On his return he was put in charge of a store and mill, in Menard County, Illinois. In 1832, at the age of twenty-three, he enlisted as a soldier in a volunteer company, going into the Black Hawk War, and was made Captain. He served three months, and on returning home was nominated for the Legislature, and in his own County, strongly opposed to him in politics, received two hundred and seventy-seven out of two hundred and eighty-four votes, though he failed of election. Then he opened a country store, which he gave up to take the office of Postmaster, and began to read law by borrowing books at night, to be returned in the morning. At the same time he bought a compass and chain, and a treatise on surveying, and became a practical surveyor. In 1834 he was elected to the Legislature of Illinois, at the age of twenty-five, and re-elected in 1836-38 and 1840. In 1836 he began to practice law, not a day too late for him, at the age of twenty-seven. He had become a man before he became a lawyer, and to that fact we owe, perhaps, the preservation, at once of the Constitution and liberty in this Republic.

In April, 1837, at the age of twenty-eight, he removed to Springfield, the capital of Illinois, where he lived twenty-four years, till he left it for the capital of the nation, as President of the United States. His success in the law was immediate and eminent, and his interest in politics did not decline. He was often candidate for Presidential elector, and became a favorite of the people, as a public speaker, as early as 1844. In 1846, at the age of thirty-seven, He was elected to Congress from Illinois. In the Congress in which he sat he was chiefly noticed for his votes in favor of liberty, and in 1849 he offered a bill for abolishing slavery in the District of Columbia. He was a member of the Convention that nominated General Taylor for the Presidency, 1848. In 1849 he was a candidate for United States Senator from Illinois. He continued in the practice of his profession till the events between 1850 and 1856 aroused him to a new interest in national politics.

He had become one of the most eminent men of a State not poor in able men, and when, in 1858, the Republican party of Illinois looked about for a rival worthy of Stephen A. Douglas, it unanimously nominated him for United States Senator. On this occasion he made that remarkable speech in which he declared that this Union must, of necessity, become "all free or all slave"--a speech which, like the famous address of Mr. Seward, at Rochester, New York, in 1858, announcing the 'irrepressible conflict' between freedom and slavery, has been so wonderfully verified by the events of the last four years. In the memorable discussion that followed between Mr. Lincoln and Mr. Douglas, the former was fairly placed before the American people as one of the ablest men of the party to which he was attached. He was defeated as candidate for the Senate, only to be nominated as candidate for President of the United States, in 1860, and in November of that year was fairly and triumphantly elected Chief Magistrate of the Republic, at the age of fifty-one.

And it was no illiterate, obscure, vulgar, county court pettifogger that was chosen by the people of the United States to this exalted position. Of course the enemies of the Republic, at home and abroad, vilified and ridiculed him as they always have hated and despised every great friend of the people. Unhappily, too many of the friends of freedom were not clear-sighted enough to recognize at once in this simple, unpretending, homely citizen, the Father of the American People.

Many doubted his capacity; others ridiculed his rhetoric and manners; others slandered his character, or denounced him as a masked friend of the despotism that was assailing the nation's life. But if all these men had reflected, they would have suspended their judgment. They would have seen that no university could have been so good a school for the man who was to defend the American People against a fierce and proud aristocracy, as just the life, which Abraham Lincoln had lived for fifty years. He had seen and he knew well all kinds of men. He was acquainted with free labor; not alone by writing elegant essays or committing to memory and reciting flowery speeches upon it, but by actively working in its every important department. He was an experienced legislator, a distinguished lawyer, a trusted political leader, only requiring opportunity to become a statesman. Mr. Seward declared, as early as 1844, that Abraham Lincoln would become one of the foremost men of the country, and his judgment was that of every man qualified to appreciate him, who was not blinded by envy or political prejudice. He was known in public and private to be a stanch friend of universal freedom. And better than this, he had lived through the toils and temptations of a new country, and come out at fifty a pure, honest, religious man.

I remember seeing his portrait presented by himself to a worthy old woman in Kentucky, after he became President, with the touching inscription, in his own hand: "In remembrance of a Bible presented to me twenty years ago by your pious hands."

He was a man in whom the people had learned to confide; and experience has proved that in the long run, the people can be trusted to select their rulers. Like the people, in all ages, his nature was slow, many-sided, often obscure and apparently contradictory in its motions, not brilliant or melodramatic, but patient, ever searching for truth, ever opening into unexpected developments of power, adequate for; all emergencies, created to separate wrong from right, and plant justice and liberty on foundations as enduring as the human race.

He rose at once to the exigency of the hour. The slave aristocracy, far more penetrating than the people, knew Abraham Lincoln for their most formidable enemy, and revolted in fury when his election was announced. For four dismal months had the work of disorganization gone on, till seven States had seceded, established a pretended government, elected a president, and enrolled an army. The government at Washington was meanwhile but a hollow name--treasonable in spirit, anxious only to compromise with rebels who threatened its own existence. Already had the dread decree gone forth among the nations, that the Union was forever gone. The North was distracted only less than the border States, all of which were on the eve of revolution.

At this gloomy hour Abraham Lincoln began his journey, on February 11, 1861, from Springfield, Illinois, to the national capital. To his friends, at parting, he said: "A duty devolves upon me, which is perhaps greater than that which has devolved upon any other man since the days of Washington. He never would have succeeded except for the aid of Divine Providence, upon which he at all times relied. I think I can not succeed without the same divine aid which sustained him, and in the same Almighty Being I place my reliance for support, and I hope you, my friends, will all pray that I may receive that divine assistance, without which I cannot succeed, but with which success is certain."

He journeyed slowly, visiting the principal cities of Indiana, Ohio and the Middle States, on his way, and speaking brief words of wisdom and conciliation to the people. We thought those little, homely, rugged speeches, unworthy then, but now we see the admirable judgment that managed to say nothing when nothing ought to be said, and to deliver great principles in the most familiar way.

Three ideas appeared prominent through all the public and private addresses of this journey: First, that salvation could come to the Republic from no man, but only from Almighty God and the American people; second, that the Union was not a "free love" arrangement, which could be dissolved or renewed at pleasure, and that the so-called doctrine of State Rights meant practically the power of any State to "rule everything below and ruin everything above it;" third, that the object of the fathers in establishing this Union was the freedom of mankind, and he, like them, was willing to work and to die for that end. In his speech at Independence Hall, in Philadelphia, as if in anticipation of his own sacrifice, he said concerning the idea which was the center of the Revolutionary war and the Declaration of Independence: "It was that which gave promise that in due time the weight should be lifted from the shoulders of all men. If this country cannot be saved without giving up that principle, I would rather be assassinated on this spot than surrender it!" Noble man! Thou hast fallen by the assassin's hand; but not till that old bell on Independence Hall has pealed out, "Liberty through all the land!"

On this journey, at Albany, N. Y., I first saw Mr. Lincoln. I saw him three times in one day--first, in the morning, in the hall of Representatives, where he delivered a few gracious words to the assembled Legislature. I remarked chiefly during his speech the depth of kindness in his grave and tender eyes, out of which looked a soul large enough to enfold all mankind. Again I saw him at noon, escorted down State Street, by a great throng of citizens, quite surrounded by a military array; he standing up at his full height in his carriage. Never had I seen, never shall I again see, so majestic a sight. I felt, as I looked on him then, that there was a man strong enough to fight secession, backed by all the powers of earth and all the demons of the infernal world. In the evening, I was glad to take his hand, which near midnight was not too wearied to give my own a grasp that made me his personal friend. Once only, afterward, did I see him--one Sunday afternoon, in Washington, the second summer of the war. He was standing on the grass before a hospital, in the suburbs, shaking hands with a long line of invalid soldiers, and talking like a father to his sons. From the hour I first saw him I believed him the man he has become.

He was wise enough to avoid assassination before his work was begun, and went to the capital in disguise. On the 4th of March 1861, with an imposing military and civic display, amid universal apprehension of danger, he was inaugurated sixteenth President of the United States.

It is not my purpose to follow Mr. Lincoln through the four years of his administration, or attempt any partisan advocacy of the civil or military policy of the Government under his lead. I know that policy has been contested honestly as well as dishonestly, often by political friends no less than by political enemies. We have not yet arrived at the historical point whence an impartial estimate can be made of its most important phases. But I may call attention to the great distinctive features by which it will be estimated in future times.

The first characteristic feature of his administration was his conviction that he was cast in a providential crisis of human affairs, and could be only a humble agent of God in a mighty work of regeneration to the Republic. No man in the Union had, from the first, a profounder sense of the vast and radical nature of the nation's conflict than Abraham Lincoln. He saw, long before the breaking forth of war, that the great American aristocracy of the South would use its institution of slavery to rule or ruin the Government, and that the attempt would result in its complete success or complete destruction. He said that Washington had not so difficult a task as himself. He saw that no party could save the Union; not even the loyal people alone; but, as he so often said. "God Almighty and the American people." He felt he was cast in one of the great eras of history. He once said to some clergymen who proposed prayer that God would come on the country's side: "Let us get on God's side, and all will be well." He knew that such a movement of national forces could neither be hastened nor hindered by mere human will, and set himself to watching the development of the mighty drama, and helping the American people keep step with the progress of Providential events. Nobody can understand this four years of his life at all who does not regard the solemn sense of being an agent of God in a great work as the back-ground of his whole policy.

The second characteristic feature of his policy was his great and unaffected faith in the loyal American people, and his belief that they were being led by God to a glorious end which they did not yet apprehend. He saw that while the slave aristocracy was fully educated down to its infamous work, the loyal American people were not yet educated up to the glorious part they were to play in this revolution of humanity. He knew they were divided by political habits, social sympathies, and often by radical ideas of society, and that no number of excellent speeches or no attempts at a dictatorship for freedom would convert his opponents. They must be brought into support of the great war of freedom by the inevitable progress of events; and he knew events would come to force them over to the side of the right. So he waited for the people to be educated into union for the sake of a Republic dedicated to freedom. From March, 1861, to January, 1863, he aided the people to wage war with a divided mind, on an enemy that knew just what he wanted, and never wavered in its support. If the result was not satisfactory, the fault was no imbecility in the Executive arm, but uncertainty in the popular mind, which was the source of all power.

It is only by referring to these two central ideas of Mr. Lincoln's policy, that any fair estimate can be made of much that has been called weak and vacillating, by those who only looked on the surface of events. And these ideas do light up the whole course of that administration which, beginning in apparent uncertainty, has gone on, like the operations of nature, to its present magnificent success.

Comforting a Nation

It is often asked, why did he not, at his inauguration, call the loyal people to arms against a treason already consummated? Because the people were not then ready to fight; but full half the community believed war could be averted by compromise. Why, then, did he not attempt compromise? Because he saw that none was possible, except one which would change the Republic to a permanent oligarchy. He waited till popular conviction demanded war, and then compelled the aristocracy to open the conflict in the most aggravating way.

Why, then, did he not call out a million men, and crush the enemy at once? Because the call for any such large number of soldiers would have astonished and divided the people, while the call that was made powerfully stimulated their patriotism. He determined that the people should make their own call for armies, for navies, for the frightful expense of war, for severe measures of martial law, for every thing essential to success. He was their servant, not their master. While, therefore, during the first year of the war, he was often accused of holding the people back, he always subtly and powerfully stimulated the public zeal, and never waited to be called twice to do a necessary thing.

Why did he appoint to the command of our largest armies, Generals who were either incompetent or unwilling to destroy the rebel hosts? and why did he retain them long after a large portion of the people lost confidence in them? Because he knew that the military and naval commanders who would finally conquer, must be educated in actual war. Not one of them had ever commanded 10,000 men, or maneuvered a fleet in action. He could only choose the generals who appeared best, give them the most generous opportunity and confidence, and wait until the real man appeared. True, some of our armies were disastrously defeated, in the summer of '61 and '62; but does any man know that they would not have been under any other commander likely then to be substituted? Did the army of the Potomac immediately succeed on the discharge of Gen. McClellan? He waited and thought and toiled, until war had educated the great leaders and the veteran host that have, within the last two years, swept the armed confederacy from the earth. Take your map of the South, and consider that on April 15th, 1861, all of it was practically in rebellion; and that on the day he died, four years later, only one small army in North Carolina stood, shaking in its shoes, the rear guard of the rebel power on its retreat to oblivion, and ask yourself sincerely if you believe any other man could have done a greater work in that time than the President of the United States? Do you say the people did it? O! that is just the point. He had aided the people to disentangle themselves from a purely peaceful civilization, and in four years become one of the most formidable military and naval powers on the globe. And history will say, never was a greater people so greatly led.

Why did he not choose better men for office? The proof of his administration is before you. You may or may not think this or that civil functionary the best, but do you doubt the great work has been done? The people of the United States have learned, under Abraham Lincoln, how to govern themselves without the aid of the slave aristocracy and its satellites. Does it matter what good man or men hold office, so that thing is done? Why did he tolerate dissensions in his Cabinet? He had far less than Washington, and like Washington, he tried to represent all great sections of the loyal people in his administration, by appropriate men. He united the people at least, whatever friction there may have been among statesmen, and however inconsistent they may have thought his course. There were never in public office in America, so many able and patriotic men as now and they were all the friends and sincere mourners of the people's President, who was the best of them all.

Why did he show such a spirit of conciliation to border States, to enemies abroad, to foes in the loyal States? Because he knew that no man loves you so much as a regenerated enemy. Because he often did thereby change the country's enemies to its friends. Because he was often compelled to endure what he could not cure. It was better to sin on the side of forbearance and patience in dealing with great States, like Kentucky and Missouri, than on the side of impatience and wrath. It was better to bear insult from foreign nations till we could speak and be respected. Was it not better to endure the folly and frenzy of sympathizers with rebellion at home than sow the seeds of implacable hatred through every neighborhood of the loyal States? Mr. Lincoln believed the Union was to stand and be a Union for Liberty, and he wisely believed the less of wrath the people had to forget the easier it would be, in the great day of reconstruction, to close up in a fellowship that should endure.

Why did he wait so long, almost two years, before he struck the decisive blow at slavery, which has gained us the victory of arms while it has saved us a free Republic? Because the people, even in January 1863, were hardly prepared for so great a challenge. Consider how you regarded slavery ten years, five years ago! It was a great divinity, against which we all dreaded to speak. We may have feared and hated it, but we kept ourselves respectful in its haughty presence. I believe the Emancipation Proclamation came not one day too late. Two years ago the children in our streets were throwing stones at colored women. He waited till slavery had taught the people its hideous nature by sending affliction into myriads of homes, and bringing the nation to death's door. So, when he did speak, a black cloud seemed to lift; and from that day our armies never lost a mile of territory really gained, and pressed on to final victory. This giant power now lies prostrate. A hundred and fifty thousand men who were slaves four years ago now carry United States muskets. The Congress of the United States has voted for, and every State will finally ratify the amendment to the Constitution that abolishes that pest forever. Is not this a success; to destroy such a huge and terrible power in five years; and will not the man who helped the people do it be called by all the holy names that mankind gives to its benefactors?

I believe history will pronounce Abraham Lincoln's administration of our Government a triumphant success. The wisest friends of the people abroad so declare it now; the wisest men in America have been growing into this conviction month by month, and the people have not doubted it from the first. Thank God, he lived to be approved by the people, and re-elected to his great station; he lived to place Grant over the army, and Farragut over the navy, and Chase at the head of the courts; lived till the confederacy had collapsed, and its President, legislature, and armies were fugitives; lived to show his enemies what he was willing to do for them. As he sat in that last cabinet meeting, the day before his death, urging a Christian clemency, and yearning to enfold every erring citizen in the arms of the Union, he was the noblest figure of this century. He was ready to be offered. Dreadful as was his departure, had it been less so, would it have startled out the wondrous love from the hearts of all men that now appears? Men who have spent their days and nights for three years in bitter hostility to his person and policy were surprised into tearful admiration and sincere eulogy. The only great State that voted against his re-election, confesses through her Governor that she has lost her best friend, and Kentucky will yet explore her mountains and dive into her mammoth caves in search of marble white enough to build his monument. Was it not better he should go on to heaven as a martyr, like Socrates, like William of Orange, like Hampden; should be one of the glorious army whose Leader died on the cross, than to die as a worn-out statesman? He died when his work was done. In his death the nation has newness of life.

Abraham Lincoln has often been contrasted with Cromwell, Napoleon, Caesar, William of Orange, Washington, Luther, and other great leaders of that stamp. He was not that kind of a leader of men. He did not lead by a display of prodigious powers in a state of splendid exhibition. He did not suck up all the vigor of a nation into himself, and use the multitudes only as tools of his imperial reason and will. The time is past, at least in this country, when such a leader can arise. No man was ever great enough to dominate over the twenty millions of freemen in our loyal States, as even Washington ruled the three millions of the first revolution. A few men during the last four years have tried to do it, but where are these men today? Jefferson Davis was the ablest leader of that sort on this continent. He succeeded in enslaving twelve millions of people for one year, and then his power began to decline, and what can he do now with his confederacy? Nothing, but get out of it as fast as steam or horseflesh can carry him. Only a profound ignorance of the character of our people and the nature of our institutions would look for a leader of this character in a revolution like the present.

But he was a leader in the people's new and improved meaning of that word. His was a vast soul all attuned to receive the noblest inspiration of a great nation's life; apt to reconcile, comprehend, combine, suggest, secure all that can be gained, strive after what should be attainable, guide and be guided by the march of events, lie open on one side to God, and on the other to the people, till the greatest ends are achieved, and all men rejoice, and each man honestly thinks himself has done it all. Is not this the perfect proof of the matchless leadership of our Lincoln, that under him the Union and freedom have been saved, and many an able, and how many an unable man shirks himself the saviour? Many a great commander thinks the army and navy have saved us? But who has been the father of all these great commanders, born like Providence with their weaknesses, healed their feuds, reconciled their quarrels, inspired them and the soldiers with increased devotion to the cause, and left us, at the end of a four years' war, with less danger of a military despotism than when it began?

Many a great statesman thinks himself and his clique have saved the country! But who has kept all these statesmen up to their duty, set them an example of self-sacrifice, purity of life, catholicity, patience, love of truth and justice? Who has cheerfully borne their insults, endured their quarrels, adjusted their rival claims, used them all, or consented to be used by any of them as the country demanded? I would derogate from no man's just claim of services, but I fancy history will paint many of these statesmen in their relation to the President as we see groups of men in the photograph standing about the trunk of the great California tree. He surpassed them all in that massive manhood, which is a perfect tower of strength in days like these.

And though the people may claim that they have done this great thing under God Almighty, yet had God denied them such a father on earth as Abraham Lincoln, I fear they would have gone on their way many years yet in the wilderness before they saw the promised land. For he it was, and none other that united and kept together the parties of which the people were composed: Republican, Democrat, Radical, Conservative; each by turn his denouncer, but every one at last his follower; he has so impressed them that they all kneel and clasp one another's hands about his bier today. And the time is yet to come when the children of the rebellious South will bless him who subdued them without ignominy; who blasted all their wild and wicked hopes, yet thereby raised them to the possibility of a new civilization.

Do you talk of such a man as simply "amiable," "goodhearted," "honest?" He was gifted with the rarest kind of greatness known in this world. He was a great, religious, philanthropic, reasonable soul, silently attracting all men to a vast good. His powers were not showy, because so massive, so like nature itself. His mind was like the nation he ruled--colossal, ever emerging into new and higher developments of life, inexhaustible in its latent capacity, crude and homely in its motions only when it was reaching out to a higher truth than has yet been organized among men. His presidency forms an era in the history of the world. Under him first has there been a prospect of a great people united to perpetuate the liberty and welfare of all men. He can wait for that nation, in some hour of its future glory, to understand fully what he was, and how he toiled, and how weary he became and how he died that it might live.

And of all the rulers of mankind, from the earliest to the latest times, who has lived a purer, more blameless life than he? He is only called a tyrant by the assassins who, failing to shoot the republic to death, wreaked their vengeance on his wearied brain. But who can lay his hand on his heart and accuse him of willful wrong? I have heard him ridiculed in certain quarters for lack of good manners. Edward Everett said he was the peer of the noblest representatives of the oldest courts of Europe.

He has been called to order for his humor and love of homely story telling. It was almost his only amusement; and if any prince, king, emperor, or president has had a more innocent way of amusing himself than Mr. Lincoln's "little stories " I have not read of it. The recreations of the great men of the earth have too often been the curse of their subjects. Can any man or woman in America say that Abraham Lincoln has indulged himself to their harm? As well might you criticize the cloudy sky for the levity of its heat lightning, as such a lofty, grave, deep, faithful soul for that playful humor that made him beloved by every child that could reach up and catch his hand as he walked the streets, and saved his powers from premature collapse.

And the grandest thing of all is he has led us up to the point where we can live without him. Why, in this hour of universal mourning, when the tears of millions flow, is the heart of the nation assured and hopeful? Why does commerce hold her sensitive scales today with steady hand? Why do we all rejoice amid our woe? The Republic has lost the friend who has taught it how to bear his loss. We shall go right on. Great duties and dangers are yet ahead; but we have learned how to meet them, and we fear no ruin. He has united the loyal North. Let that North not give way now to the voice of wrath and pagan vengeance, but live and act in his lofty spirit, and all men in this broad land shall finally gather about his feet in unity.

Far in the East lies the grave of George Washington, which no sound of war has disturbed.

That turf is hallowed ground. To all those thousands who have fought along the Potomac, the Rappahannock and the James, his has been the one remaining honored name--Father of his Country.

In the far West, today we build the tomb of Abraham Lincoln. We bury him now as Washington was buried, with thousands of enemies. But time will abolish them all, and year-by-year the prairies will be thronged by pilgrims to his resting place, till all know him, as the Father of the American People, and the American people are one.

A Collection of Sermons

Rev. Henry E. Parker
April 16, 1865

DISCOURSE

THE DAY AFTER THE

RECEPTION OF THE TIDINGS

OF THE ASSASSINATION OF

PRESIDENT LINCOLN,

PREACHED IN THE

South Congregational Church,

CONCORD, N. H., APRIL 16, 1865.

BY THE PASTOR,
REV. HENRY E. PARKER.

DISCOURSE.
JOHN 11: 53.
"Then from that day forth they took counsel together for to put him to death."

It is no new thing for the good to be hated, and to be martyred. Eighteen hundred years ago a Divine One walked the earth; yet he had bitter enemies, who foully plotted against his life; nor did their malice subside till their fiendish machinations were successful; with a traitor's aid they compassed his death one Friday afternoon in April, or the month most nearly corresponding to it in the Jewish Calendar. That day has been remembered. A large part of the Christian world annually commemorate it with enjoined fastings and penitential sorrow. Day before yesterday was its anniversary; the day once made dark with the crucifixion. It is by a strange permission of Providence that henceforth the American mind will associate with Good Friday and its dying Lord, the death of our honored President. Providence has permitted the singular coincidence, sad and sacred. Nor was it any dishonor to thee, President Lincoln, to have fallen by the hand of such an assassin--the victim of such malice. The friendship of such men would have been a dishonor--men in whose hearts was still rampant the demon of secession and rebellion. This is not the first case where hatred, and wrong, and violence, have been an eternal honor to him who has experienced them. Thine assassination by Secessia's hand is the very crown of thy patriotism and worth!

And murder, murder just like this, horrible as hell could conceive, which has stunned the nation this day, which will shock the world, we had, perhaps, full reason to expect. When, four years ago this last fall, the votes of the nation declared to the South that they could no longer rule the country, that their power had departed, then were formed plots to seize upon the government by violence, and prevent the rightful occupant from ever reaching the Presidential Chair. "Then from that day forth they took counsel together for to put him to death." We well remember how, only through the adroit management of friendly railroad officials, the President reached Washington at all. We could not believe it till the fact was forced upon us, that there was a definite, well-laid plan to assassinate him on the way; and that leading southern men were both cognizant of the plot and accessory to it. We know, however, that for a long time guards were felt to be necessary about the Presidential mansion. We know how that, from time to time, discoveries were made of new plots, requiring new precautions. We remember how, when for health's sake the President had retired to the "Soldiers' Retreat" as a summer residence, it was found requisite for his safety that he should be daily accompanied in and out from Washington with a mounted escort. The threats of the dangers of assassination thus have always hung about him.

Or is it surprising that the black heart and bloody hand of the genius of slavery and rebellion should have been equal to an act like this; the pitiless heart, the savage hand, long familiar with lacerating the naked bodies of bondmen and bondwomen, tearing husbands and wives asunder, parents and children;--that black heart which could nourish treason such as this rebellion has brought forth, how natural a nest for such a project of assassination! That matricidal hand lifted against the mother country of us all --how slight a thing for it to wield the assassin's weapons! And when, by the recent victories, it had at last become evident to the blindest southern pride and hate that the miserable cause of the Confederacy was meeting its miserable end, then, stung to madness in its disappointed rage, this act is most naturally committed: like the devils of the bottomless pit, ruined themselves, their only remaining care to ruin as much with them as possible. I know of no parallel out of hell. The nearest to it in human history is the act of Herod, who, when he knew that he must die, incarcerated the most eminent citizens of the realm, with strict orders for their assassination at the moment of his death, that there might be some mourning in the land. Oh that it had been the will of heaven in like manner to have frustrated this infernalism as it did that!

Yes, we had reason enough to infer this act, but it had been deferred so long we fondly hoped that safety was secured. Alas! How terribly were we

mistaken! Oh, my country, my country! How have I, in these late years, mourned for thee in thy prostration in the dust!--at the humiliating spectacle thou has made for the derision of the nations--who thy struggles and thy sorrows--who have mocked at thy departing greatness and glories, as they hoped; who have looked upon thy gigantic efforts against thy foe, thy wounds and thy blood, as the degenerate thousands of the ancient amphitheater stretched their eager necks, and with fiendish satisfaction gloated over the struggling gladiators of the arena,
"Butchered to make a Roman holiday!"

And now, when at last I saw thee, my noble country, emerging from thy humiliation and disgrace, and springing to shine old position of influence and renown, and more, --Oh, to see thee present this most humbling sight of all before the world, of having nourished such a monster, capable of such an act, and of having such a deed committed upon thy soil! For, excepting the murder of the ages, the crucifixion itself, human history seems not to have furnished its parallel.

But, my hearers, are there any words to be uttered this hour, beside those of bitter lamentation for the act and execration of it? Can I today perform my usual duty of uttering God's lessons to you, as suggested by the volume of his word or the book of his providence? Sufficient time has not yet elapsed to enable us to recover from the appalling, bewildering effects of the tidings. We cannot yet look upon the matter with a clear and steady eye. Still, I feel there are some things I can even now say.

And, first: I feel that we are more than ever in God's hands; that he is most directly and conspicuously dealing with us. Think of our feelings the past two weeks till yesterday. There were no bounds to our joy--we could not express it! And how that joy brought the nation in gratitude to God; the nation never so acknowledged him in any joy. Every speech that was made did it; men did it one with another; men who seldom spoke his name felt then they must speak of him; where men gathered in the business mart, and on the exchange, doxologies must be sung, and prayer and the devout offering of thanksgiving be made. I am so glad God was thus acknowledged; not indeed as he ought to have been, but yet as he never was before, it gives us such ground for trusting that this terrible thing is something other than a divine rebuke. And now our sorrow is as great as was then our joy. The very greatness of these extremes in the permissions of God's providence, are a proof that he is as signally with us. It is not in wrath; it is not in divine desertion that we are experiencing this. The magnitude of the previous mercy shows this. That was in one sense a gracious preparation for this; and we have still all our late successes and victories to lean upon to strengthen and support us.

It is possible that without great and increasing elation, there may have been some danger that we should come to lose our sense of dependence--come to feel as though all our troubles were past, no more dangers to fear, and so soon become God-forgetting and self-sufficient. I do not know; perhaps God saw this was about to be--and he anew humbled us, and taught us, right in the midst of our highest joy, that without his preservation, every cup of our hopes and satisfactions will be dashed.

Long ago I learned to feel that the more striking the events in our personal experience, the more evidently God is dealing with us as individuals. I do not know why I should have any less strong convictions when applying the rule to national events.

II. But I see more clearly the hand and the mercy of God in not allowing this event to occur until it did. Had the first intentions of assassination, and the first attempts four years ago been successful, it is difficult to say how dire might have been the results. Anarchy, very likely, would have sprung upon us at once. Our institutions, our circumstances, certainly then could not have borne such a trial, so critical a test as they can now; or if the event had occurred at any time subsequently until the present. And think what an interposition of the divine goodness we ought to call it, and most in the loyal States will call it, that the President was not taken away before completing the great acts of his administration, especially the two which have most signalized it, the bringing an end to slavery and to the rebellion.

III. Another thought which presents itself is, that perhaps this last act was needed to complete the infamy of the rebellion and secession, and of that nefarious system of human servitude out of which secession and rebellion grew. Such an act as this is the legitimate offspring of those monsters, and nothing else. It is the very hard-hearted pitilessness and savagery of slavery, which can thus wrest the life of the devoted husband from directly beneath the eyes of the loving wife, and tear the life of the fond father directly from the embraces of dear children; slavery can educate to such bloody heartlessness. It was the hand of rebellion and secession that first recklessly and ruthlessly snatched war's flaming brand and waved it challengingly and defiantly in the eyes of this government and this nation; and it is the same hand of revolting and appalling recklessness and crime which has now seized the assassin's weapons, and, after with one of them murdering the defenseless man, the husband, the father, the President, waved the other with that tragic style and devil's heroism which have characterized the actors in the rebellion all along. Perhaps this last consummating act was needed to open fully the eyes of foreign nations sympathizing with secession to the true animus of the rebellion. I doubt if we hear any more commendations of it, or apologies for it; it will at last have succeeded in awakening the detestation and abhorrence of the civilized world, as it long ago should have done.

And I am not sure but that we too needed this further deed of horror to be done, that we might be preserved from all false leniency toward that trio of abominations, slavery, secession, and rebellion; that we might at once proceed with unsparing and speedy hand to root out every vestige of them. I have of late feared much lest their downfall should not be stamped with sufficient ignominy for the best instruction and safeguard of coming generations. There is little fear now, however.

At the outset of this rebellion I, in this house, laid the charge and crime of it at the door of slavery! Little did I think, that in its closing hours such a final illustration of its general character and leadings would be furnished. But this foul, fell act comes from the same influences which could lead, ten years ago, to that brutal, murderous beating of the Massachusetts senator, defenseless in his legislative seat; which four years ago could fiendishly fling the horrors of civil war into this land of happiness and peace; which afterward could wretchedly imitate that miserable villain of two hundred and sixty years ago, Guy Faux, and mine the Libby Prison to destroy, at a single explosion, our prisoners, if Capt. Dahlgren should seek to liberate them, and then, subsequently, without shame, justify the act; and which could deliberately starve so many thousands of our poor captive soldiers, if to death they did not care, out of all possible future serviceableness to their country they meant, if not to death; this last work of horrid assassination is but the latest. God grant it the final flowering of the same hellish plant!

IV. And not only may this foul deed have been needed to put the last possible brand of infamy upon the rebellion and its primal cause, but it also may have been desirable as the final, highest test of the strength of our institutions and form of government. The rebellion and its subjugation have been a fearful but most triumphant test; this is a further, in the view of some it would be even a severer. In other lands the assassination of the chief ruler has perhaps usually been the precursor of anarchy and revolution. Wisely was it that not four hours were suffered to elapse before our Vice-President was sworn into the office of President. As foreign nations see us pass through the ordeal of the termination of one President's career by violence, and the immediate introduction to the office of his successor, without commotion, and the continuance of each department and office of the government without any infringement upon the usual order and routine, it may be regarded as under God the last, highest test of the sufficiency of our Republican form of institutions for any and all emergencies.

V. Again, it may be observed, that very possibly the work of President Lincoln was now done, so far as he could complete it. Very possibly another could better take it up and carry it on. He has done a great work--a marvelous work; history will record it as of unsurpassed magnitude and honor. He could not have added to his fame. The remaining work is now that of reconstruction, and the meting out the best measure of blended clemency and justice to those who have been traitors and rebels. Very possibly a southern loyal man may know better their true spirit and deserts, and decide upon the better course of treatment with respect to them. To us, indeed, it seems as though Mr. Lincoln could carry on the remaining work better than any other; yet it may be otherwise. To us, it seems, at the least, a fearful experiment to turn from the always discreet, self-poised, temperate and sober man, to put the highest authority of this government into the hands of a man who has so recently and unutterably disgraced himself and us through him. But if the imposing upon him this great burden of responsibility shall have the same effect the similar imposing of a similarly weighty responsibility is said to have had upon the great Lieutenant-General of our armies, he has abundant talents, knowledge and experience for the position. God keep him and bless him. God bless President Johnson! My own conviction is that he will better complete what Mr. Lincoln has so incomparably thus far carried on, than even our lamented late President himself, if spared, would.

VI. Yet again, it may be observed, that this fearful event will have a mighty and happy tendency to unite our people. It is not going to have the effect of throwing us into anarchy, or of confusing any of the operations of our government, or retarding at all the progress of our triumphant quelling of the rebellion, as perhaps the perpetrator of this crime and his associates imagined. It will be a new and signal illustration of the folly of revenge. This act will utterly destroy what little remaining sympathy there was in any quarter for the falling cause of the confederacy. It will establish an ineradicable aversion toward it in the breasts of all right-minded men, of all patriots, of all lovers of law and order, of all friends of their fellow men, of all desiring the welfare of mankind. He had centered upon him those animosities every where felt toward those who stood by our government; those animosities, to a great extent, will be buried with him;--while even where, to any extent, they may partially or temporarily remain, his sad and wicked end will greatly soften and ameliorate them. Diversities of political views and feelings can be no longer violently cherished over such a grave; we shall all together deprecate the deed; and the causes which led to it. There are none of us, I think, who will go forward to our work and duties as citizens of this Republic any the worse for going on more soberly and sadly. This event falls most exactly in the line of God's dealing with us ever since the commencement of our difficulties, by never letting us long rest in our dependence on any individual. He has signally disappointed us in this respect, by death and otherwise, and utterly defeated all our tendencies to the adulation of any one. It seems to be his great purpose thus, as in other ways, that, under him, our people must look to themselves for the accomplishing what they need and desire. It is a great effort of his providence to elevate and strengthen the individual sense of duty and obligation among all the people. It is a republicanizing and democratizing of the people on a plane of elevation and importance in advance of every thing thus far in our national experience and character.

But most imperfectly can our poor discernment now interpret the lessons of this event. Let us at least "humble ourselves under the mighty hand of God, that he may exalt us in due time" from the dust of our present abasement and sorrow. Let us together give our united, undying enmity to those great causes and evils which have culminated in this final crime. Let us give ourselves anew to the love and service of our country, on whose altar such sacrifices have been laid. Let us in the presence of such a death realize anew the old-urged truth that no position gives immunity from the grave, and that every life hastens speedily to render its account to God.

And now rest thee, thou man beloved by more hearts and more beloved than any man in this nation before, and by none more than the dusky race, who will ever hail thee as their deliverer from bondage; thou man--mercifully raised up by heaven for the fearful crisis of our times--singularly endowed, doubtless, with the qualities most needed for the peculiar and arduous position to which thou wast called--by turns doubted of by every class and party, but in the end centering upon thyself more regard and confidence by far than any other;--thou kindly-hearted man, incapable of malice or ill-will long retained, thy very genialness and humor, a gift sustaining thee, perhaps, when others would have sunk beneath depression and care;--thou man of the people--thou perfect representative of the character and the admirableness of our institutions, which can elevate the humblest and the poorest to the loftiest position among us, and fit worthily and well to fill it; thou wouldst not thyself have regretted that thy blood should mingle with that of the myriad patriot heroes, the victims of the spirit and deed of this rebellion--one affluent more of that mighty tide of blood ransoming our land;--how much better thy dead and mutilated form to the living form of the now fugitive head of the rebellion;--thou diest, a nation bending over thee in sorrow and in love;--he lives, a nation's execrations following him for evermore!--rest thee, worn and weary with the cares of State in most unprecedented burden, our need and our perils imposed on thee--well and bravely hast thou borne the burden, untiringly, uncomplainingly; and now thou hast laid it off; not too soon for thee, we pray it may not be too soon for us!--the last, greatest murder of the rebellion, the last, greatest sacrifice for us;--the hatred of our enemies toward us laid on thee--their venom concentrated upon thee--their malice, by the most detestable of crimes, wreaking a coveted, cowardly vengeance;--bearing so much, suffering so much, and at last thus murdered, simply because thou wert our President, sustaining, directing, defending, delivering our government;--rest thee now from thy great and weary world! History will give thee a high and spotless fame; it will record thee as one of the most amiable and unexceptionable of men, as one of the truest and noblest of patriots, as one of the wisest and ablest of Presidents,--rest thee in the Republic's undying honor, reverence, gratitude and love--and may a Redeemer's advocacy and blood crown thy soul with celestial glory, immortal happiness, and everlasting life!

Rev. Cephas B. Crane
April 16, 1865

SERMON

ON THE

OCCASION OF THE

DEATH OF PRESIDENT LINCOLN.

PREACHED IN THE

SOUTH BAPTIST CHURCH, HARTFORD, CONN.,

SUNDAY, APRIL 16, 1865.

BY REV. C. B. CRANE.

2 SAMUEL, 1: 19. "THE BEAUTY OF ISRAEL IS SLAIN UPON THE HIGH PLACES; HOW ARE THE MIGHTY FALLEN!"

The nation is weeping today; and its temples and homes and places of business and public edifices are draped in mourning. Strong men, who could endure the shock of personal calamity and the pangs of personal bereavement with uncomplaining fortitude, are shaken by the violence of their emotions, and their tears fall upon the pavement of the crowded street. Gentle women, secluding themselves at home, mourn as for a husband or a lover. The festivities of society are checked, and plans for future gayety are stopped in their process of relaxation. Over the whole American sky are clouds and thick darkness. Threnodies are sung by quivering lips and wail from melancholy organs. All sounds are dirges, and the countenance of sorrow is adorned with the jewelry of tears. Oh, friends, on the evening of Good Friday, the memorial day of the crucifixion of our Lord, our good, true-hearted, magnanimous, supremely loyal, great President was smitten down by the hand of the assassin; and yester morn, at twenty-two minutes past seven of the clock, his noble and holy soul went up from its shattered and desecrated tabernacle to its God.

The terrible tragedy is consummated, its heartrending denouncement has transpired, there can be no revision of it, it stands the blackest page save one in the history of the world. It is the after-type of the tragedy, which was accomplished on the first Good Friday, more than eighteen centuries ago, upon the eminence of Calvary in Judea.

Yes, it was meet that the martyrdom should occur on Good Friday. It is no blasphemy against the Son of God and the Savior of men that we declare the fitness of the slaying of the Second Father of our Republic on the anniversary of the day on which he was slain. Jesus Christ died for the world; Abraham Lincoln died for his country. The consecration of Jesus to humanity began in the antiquity of eternity, and found its culmination when he cried with white, yet triumphant, lips, on the cross, "it is finished." The consecration of Abraham Lincoln to the American people had its phenomenal and most manifest beginning in the summer of 1858, when he entered upon that memorable Senatorial Campaign in which, while he sustained a technical defeat, he gained a substantial victory; it found its culmination on the evening of the fourteenth day of April, 1865, when the sharp pistol report announced with terrible inarticulateness, "it is finished."

And let it not grieve us overmuch, beloved brethren that the conscious life of our late honored President ceased in the theatre of our National Capital. He was there, not for the purpose of gratifying himself, but at a personal sacrifice, and for the sake of the people whom he loved. For this is the statement of the public prints: "The President and Mrs. Lincoln did not start for the theatre until fifteen minutes after eight o'clock. Speaker Colfax was at the White House at the time, and the President stated to him that he was going; although Mrs. Lincoln had not been well, because the papers had announced that General Grant and they would be present, and as General Grant had gone North he did not wish the audience to be disappointed. He went with apparent reluctance, and urged Mr. Colfax to go with him; but that gentleman had made other arrangements, and, with Mr. Ashmun of Massachusetts, bade him Good Bye." He did not wish the audience to be disappointed,"--this was the reason of his presence at the theatre on that fateful evening; and the sentiment which dictated the words has given character to all his private and public life.

One year ago the eighteenth day of next month it was my privilege to meet President Lincoln in the executive chamber of the White House, in company with a delegation from the Methodist General Conference, then in session in Philadelphia. I remember that in replying to the address which was read to him he expressed in a most devout manner his gratitude to God for giving to the government the sympathy and support of the churches. And here are words which I wrote soon after the interview, and which I repeat to you in order that you may know the impression which the personal presence of the man produced upon me: "The President looks thin and care-worn. I believe with all my heart that he bears this great nation like a burden on his life. God strengthen and guide him!"

I saw many senators at that time, and many of the representatives in Congress, and the heads of some of the departments; and I recollect that while many of them were rubicund and jovial, and others showed in their countenances only the resultant fatigue of their labor,-the form of the President was bowed as by the superimposition of a crushing load, his flesh was wasted as by the consuming flames of incessant solicitude, and his face was thin and furrowed and pale as though it had become spiritualized by the vicarious pain which he endured in bearing in himself the calamities of his country.

And just that suffering, worn, martyr-like form and face of his which I looked upon a little less than one year ago; just that unselfish love and sympathy for others which expressed itself in every lineament and gesture;-interpret to me the self-denying presence at the theatre, on the night of his immolation, of the noble Atlas on whose shoulders for four bloody years our political world has rested.

Oh memorable Good Friday, henceforth a day of sad reminiscences in the calendar of country as well as church! While I was walking the last evening but one under the solemn stars, all ignorant of the disastrous presence of the destroying angel in the land, and the tardy moon was peering over the eastern horizon as if reluctant to look upon the infernal deed which was accomplishing, two fiends in the guise of men, or two maniacs whose insanity is a crime, the creatures of the ghastly rebellion which has reared its horrid front in the South and has had shameful affiliation with dastardly reptiles of the North, were finishing, each his own hideous work, in our nation's capital The one was permitted by an inscrutable Providence in the presence of a crowded assembly to consummate his purpose upon the life of him whom the world was delighting to honor. The other, with a daring which is well-nigh unparalleled, overthrowing all who resisted his progress, forced his way into the chamber of the Secretary of State who was slowly recovering from recent injuries, and plunged the fierce knife again and again into his neck, that column which sustained as royal a brain as the present age possesses.

God's lightning, speeding along the wires, has since told us that the President is dead; and that the life of Secretary Seward hangs upon a thread which the gentlest strain would break.

Night of crime and horrors! What pen can write thy cursed record!

Friends, we will not forget to pray to God for the life of our Secretary of State; we will not forget to implore God to be a Husband to the widow and a Father to the fatherless; -but there is one form, lying in state in the nation's chamber of love, upon which all our eyes do bend in inexpressible grief.

Ah, how does the splendid life of him who was the beauty of our national Israel, unveil itself now before us, which we may appreciate how much we have lost.

We remember his obscure birth in Hardin County, Kentucky. We remember how at eight years of age his sturdy arms swung the axe in the forests of Indiana; and how the next ten years of his life were mostly occupied in hard labor on his father's farm, and how he attended school at intervals, amounting in the aggregate to only a year, which was all the school education he ever received. We remember how at the age of nineteen he floated down the Mississippi river on a flatboat to New Orleans. We remember his removal with his father, at the age of twenty-one, to Illinois, and his helping to build a log cabin for the family home, and his making enough rails to fence ten acres of land. We hear the sounding strokes of his hammer as he assisted in the building of a flatboat, which he afterwards navigated down the "Father of waters" to its mouth. We see him superintending a store and a mill, alert to improve every opportunity for advancement in life. We remember his volunteering for the Black Hawk war and his unexpected election to the captaincy of his company. We remember his borrowing law-books from a neighboring attorney, which he took in the evening and returned in the morning, studying while others slept. We remember how the surveyor of his county offered to depute to him a portion of his work, and how he procured a treatise on surveying and a compass and chain, and did the work. We remember his rapid rise to distinction in the profession, which he had chosen. We remember his election to the lower house of Congress in 1846, and his inflexible, though not factious, opposition to slavery during his entire term of service. We remember his magnificent Senatorial Campaign against Mr. Douglass, and his advocacy of truths, which became thenceforth clearer and dearer to every lover of human freedom. We remember his election to the chief magistracy of the American republic in the fall of 1860. We remember the earnest and tender appeals, which he made to his misguided brethren of the South in his first inaugural address. We remember the sagacity, which has uniformly characterized his conduct of the government through the past four years of its peril. We remember how long he subordinated his instincts against oppression to his convictions of constitutional guarantees. We remember his reluctance to issue the proclamation of Emancipation, and the entire fidelity with which he has since adhered to its provisions. We remember the magnanimous words, which he spoke to those who announced to him his nomination for the Presidency. We remember the total absence of personal triumph and of malevolence against his foes and ours, which distinguished his second inaugural. And we remember--for it is a thing of yesterday--the yearning of his great, brotherly heart toward the people of the insurgent states so soon as their capital was taken and their only formidable army was either captured or destroyed.

Oh, friends, our loss is irreparable. His heart was a woman's heart. His genius belonged to the philosopher; his intellect belonged to the statesman. The caution, which used to vex us who were more eager than wise, was the child of a tender heart and a sagacious brain. When in the depot of his own city, whence he was just setting forth to enter upon the duties of his high office, he asked for the prayers of his townsmen, he gave token of being possessed of that kind of soul which is receptive of the inspiration of the Almighty; and that God who raised him up for this critical period of our national history has inspired him for the successful accomplishment of the stupendous work which was committed to his hands.

A rare man was our martyred President, a rare character was his. Such was his greatness, that our wisest men are fearful of trusting any other hands than his at the helm of our ship of state. Such was the affection which his gentleness awakened, that women wept yesterday as though their babes had perished, and little children bore the news of his death to their parents in tears.

And can not we say together today: more blessed is Abraham Lincoln, who was slain on Friday night, than is Jefferson Davis, who, if he escape the hand of human justice, must skulk through the world with the crime of treason upon his heart and the mark of Cain upon his brow and the maledictions of futurity upon his memory forever.

Wherever the body of Abraham Lincoln shall be buried, there will be established a national shrine which shall share the honor of pilgrimages with the tomb of the illustrious hero who sleeps his long sleep amid the classic shades of Mount Vernon. Rest henceforth in peace ye ashes of our glorified patriots! Commune ye now in the land of spirits, oh elected souls of God!

But, friends, it is time that I should turn away from him who has so long fascinated to himself my thoughts and words. The eulogy of our departed father and friend, which you required of me, has been pronounced. My grief, which yesterday found only partial gratification in my tears, is further soothed by the tribute of affection, which I have now publicly paid to the beloved and honored dead.

But there remains for me a duty to you who hear me. God visits no such providence, smites with no such smiting, as this, without a reason and purpose. Is it immodest in me to assume that it is my office to voice your inquiries after the meaning of this mournful event?

(1.) Observe, then, that we needed just this,

perhaps, not only to learn the hideous enormity of the slave-holders' rebellion and of all sympathy with it from every quarter, but also for the sufficient atonement for it and proper settlement of it. Treason, murder, assassination, and all mentionable crimes, are the woof, which has from the first been woven into the warp of this gigantic and infernal rebellion. Disregard of human life, contempt for the divine authority which is vested in human rulers, supreme disdain of one who has risen from the obscurest condition to the highest office of state, eagerness to smite down the man who has been smitten by the bullet of the desperado,--all these are the legitimate fruitage of the barbarous institution of slavery which has risen against the national life. The horrible crime of Friday night has taught us that root and stem and branch of the rebellion are accursed, that there is nothing supremely abominable and devilish of which it is not capable. Every man, together with every woman, of the North, who has hitherto launched fiercer invectives against the government and its friends than against the spurious confederacy and its friends, and who does not from this day eat the hellish words which he has spoken and repent of his well-nigh unpardonable sin, is an abandoned traitor, and deserves to be hanged ten thousand times higher than Haman, and to sink ten thousand times deeper into the pit than he. His sin, if it shall continue, is sin against light clearer than noonday, and is capable of no extenuation.

But not only does the tragic event which we are commemorating betoken the fiendish nature of the rebellion; it was needed also, perchance, for the sufficient atonement for it, and proper settlement of it. If I am unwittingly blasphemous, forgive me,--but when God would bring an apostate humanity into reconciliation with himself, the sacrifice of his only and well-beloved Son was requisite to the realization of his purpose and desire.

So, when our national government would bring back to allegiance to itself its millions of apostate subjects, it was requisite that he who was dearest to all loyal hearts should be offered in sacrifice. We .had already given our treasure, and our husbands and fathers and brothers and sons. They had been laid upon the altar and were consumed. We thought our offering was costly enough, and that none costlier would be demanded. But there was a man, occupying the highest office of state, dear to all loyal hearts, the nation's father and brother and son, more anointed than any other with the holy chrism of a great people's love. The government was upon his shoulders, but he must be, nevertheless, yea, because of his office, the lamb of sacrifice.

There is a Roman legend that the ground in the middle of the Forum sank down to an immense depth, leaving a chasm, which could not be filled. At last the soothsayers declared that if the Roman Empire was to endure, that must be devoted to the chasm, which constituted the principal strength of the Roman people. When all shrank back aghast, Marcus Curtius, a noble youth, knowing that courage and consecration to country were the strength of the empire, armed himself in complete armor, mounted his horse, and leaped into the abyss. Lo, the yawning jaws of the earth came together with a shock and Rome was saved.

Is it hard for you to believe, my friends, that if we could have overheard the secret prayers of Abraham Lincoln, we might have listened to such words as these, "Oh, God, use me as thou wilt for the salvation of my beloved country?" Just that prayer from the best beloved man of the nation God may have waited for long: just that prayer he answered on Good Friday night. God accepted the costly and self-devoted sacrifice, which we had not dreamed of offering. The "Lo I come to do thy will, oh God," which fell from the lips of Jesus when he made himself the Lamb of sacrifice for the restoration of an apostate humanity to allegiance to the divine government, fell not sacrilegiously from the lips of our late heroic President when he consecrated himself to his country and became the requisite sacrifice for the restoration of rebellious citizens to allegiance to just authority.

And as the tragedy of the cross has startled tens of thousands of sinners into a recognition of their sins, while it expressed the inflexibility of God's law and authority, so we may hope that the tragedy of last Friday night will startle multitudes of rebels, North as well as South, into a recognition of their crime, stiffen the government, which might otherwise bend, into requisite rigidness, and hasten the consummation of peace for which we devoutly pray.

The last and costliest offering which God demanded has been taken; and as on the first Good Friday peace was secured between an apostate race and God, so we will trust that on the last Good Friday peace was secured between the contending regions of our distracted country.

(2.) If your meditations have been like mine, friends, you have already framed a second inquiry. Who are responsible for the assassination of Abraham Lincoln, and who share the guilt? The question, which I have asked, I dare answer. I have already shown that the open enemy are responsible, and share the guilt. But this is not the whole answer. The event about which our thoughts and regrets cluster was, partly at least, the result of a false opinion which has been industriously promulgated, and of a diabolical sentiment which has been generated, in almost every community of the North. That opinion is that the President of the Republic was a tyrant who ought to be resisted and overthrown. That sentiment is unappeasable and pitiless hatred of him.

Now it will doubtless prove that the assassin of Abraham Lincoln, although used as a tool by our

Southern enemies, was not merely a hireling, but one who had been brought to believe that the execution of his purpose would be an act alike of patriotism and piety. When he leaped upon the stage of the theatre, crying "sic semper tyrannis," "be it ever thus with tyrants," it was evident that he believed himself to have accomplished a truly just and heroic deed.

If, now, you inquire who is directly responsible for the assassination of Good Friday night, I answer, that in addition to our enemies in the South, it is those men of the North who promulgated the false opinion and generated the infernal sentiment to which I have alluded above, and which made the assassin the fanatic and monomaniac that he is. And if you ask who share the guilt of the horrible crime, which we are considering, I answer, that it is every man and woman who has shared the above-mentioned opinion and sentiment. They share the guilt, though their influence may not have extended far enough to participate in the criminal act, just as sinners today share the guilt of the crucifixion of Christ.

Let me particularize. All those editors of political papers who during the last Presidential campaign declared over and over again that Abraham Lincoln was a tyrant worthy of universal execration: all those demagogues who trumpeted the same falsehood in the ears of fierce and ignorant mobs: that man of New Haven, who asked in a public harangue, "who is the greatest traitor, Jefferson Davis or Abraham Lincoln?" that man of Hartford, who, if rumor be true, at the breaking out of the rebellion invested a thousand dollars in South Carolina bonds, in token of his sympathy with the crime of treason: that man who once held office in the President's cabinet, and who has never since broken his infamous silence except to malign the government which protected instead of hanging him: these are the men who share the responsibility of the murder of Abraham Lincoln. They helped to produce the opinion and sentiment, which produced the man who did the deed. Blood is upon their souls. Wash they their hands never so much, as did Pontius Pilate, they can never be made clean.

Shall I also particularize those who share, not the responsibility, but the guilt, of the murder of Good Friday night? I answer, all those obscure and influential men who have shared the opinion and sentiment, which I have mentioned, but who have not been capable of extensively promulgating them. That alderman in our city government who said yesterday, "I have been waiting four years for some damned black republican bones, to make bone dust to put around my vines, and I don't know but there is a prospect of my getting some now." That man, those men indeed, who were guilty of the substantial, if not the identical, expression, "I am glad that Abraham Lincoln was shot, and I would like to go down and dance on his coffin." That employee of the Springfield and New Haven railroad who expressed joy at the murder of

Mr. Lincoln, and remarked that "he ought to have been shot four years ago." Every man who has felt a secret joy at the horrible tragedy of the night before the last.

Every man who has not been carrying a mourning heart all yesterday and today.

Shall I include any women in this infamous catalogue? Women who ought to share the sweetness and tenderness of womanhood? I will not dishonor the mother who bore me by bringing so horrible a charge against her sex. But if I could speak to all the women of the land I would say, if you have ever thought or felt murder against Abraham Lincoln, the event of last Friday night is the voice of God calling you to repent in dust and ashes. And if it be true, as is reported, that a woman, whose name I do not know, said yesterday, that "she was glad Abraham Lincoln was shot, and she hoped Jefferson Davis might assume his place," I can say that rather than meet her in the way I would be confronted by all the raging Furies of Tartarus. Oh, woman! as thou canst be most tender and forgiving, so canst thou be most vindictive and implacable.

Thus I have shown you who they are who share the responsibility of the assassination of Abraham Lincoln, and who they are who share only the guilt. There is a proper attitude toward these men, which we have not yet assumed. Friendship, fraternization, forbearance with them, should cease till they purge themselves of their crime. The lines must be drawn, and even households be divided if necessary, as our Savior has predicted. Toleration of traitors and murderers and makers of murderers is not a virtue, it is a vice. The wine of our national life must become pure by separating itself from the lees of disloyalty. I have shown you the men, friends, deal with them as you will.

(3.) One other thought remains to be expressed, a thought of consolation for the future.

We have lost our Palinurus, our helmsman, and our ship of state is adrift on a stormy sea. Has God no greater Elisha to succeed the departed Elijah? Must we despair of reaching the haven of a victorious and holy peace?

All yesterday and today I have been comforting myself with the reflection that God is alive and on the throne. The Christian men and women whom I have met have lifted faces to heaven upon which was the expression of holy trust and serenity.

Although we were not aware of it, we have been for a considerable time past placing our confidence in our lamented President rather than in our God. And since his second inauguration, on which occasion Andrew Johnson brought shame upon himself and the nation, we have come almost to believe that the destiny of our country was suspended upon the single life of Abraham

Lincoln.

God has smitten down him upon whom our faith was impiously reposed, in order that he might transfer our faith to himself. And in one short hour he has accomplished what he undertook. There is not a Christian man before me, nor in the whole broad land, who has not leaned more heavily upon God, and been more consciously sustained, during yesterday and today, than for months before. We recognize our need of the divine arm, and lo, we feel ourselves embraced by it and upheld.

More than this, I believe that God purposes to bring final deliverance to the republic by the same Andrew Johnson in whom on the fourth day of last March we lost faith. Not only was the man whom we trusted taken away, but the man whom we distrusted is made the captain of our hosts. Him will God anoint for our salvation.

For, friends, I know that God will save this nation. Our whole history, and especially the history of the last four years, would be nothing else than an excrescence upon the trunk of time, if we should not reach a higher national perfection and prosperity than we have yet realized.

And since I know that the republic will be delivered, I have all faith that Andrew Johnson will be used for the accomplishment of our deliverance.

True, he stumbled fearfully at the start. But there has been wrought a marvelous change in the man during the forty-one days which have since elapsed. If that maudlin speech of his in the Senate chamber on the fourth of March was a disgrace to himself and to the nation, his speech yesterday on the occasion of taking the oath of the Presidential office, and his manly, yet humble and devout bearing, more than atoned for the earlier folly.

Do you not remember how we lost faith in Gen. Ulysses Grant at the bloody battle of Pittsburg Landing, and afterward during the siege of Vicksburg? But he was God's anointed man, and today we esteem him second to no captain whom the world has produced.

Do you not remember how our confidence in Abraham Lincoln was shaken when he went from Springfield to Washington, making little speeches from the platform of the car all the way. Today we lament him as one of the greatest statesmen whom history celebrates.

And it is a singular fact that during this great conflict those men, of whom we had the highest hopes at the beginning of their career, have signally failed; while they whom at the outset we distrusted, have attained to preeminent success.

And so my faith in God's using of Andrew Johnson

for our national salvation is all the greater because the beginning of his more exalted career was so inauspicious.

But there is another phase of the general thought, which we are considering to which I invite your attention. Abraham Lincoln's work is done. Therefore, we can say, since God is in this thing, that on the evening of the fourteenth day of the present April his work was done. From that time God had no further use for him in the position which he held. At that time God had use for Andrew Johnson in the place which was left vacant.

Can we not detect some reasons for this providence of God?

It seems plain to me that our late President was peculiarly adapted to the work which he has accomplished, and to the past phases of the great conflict which is now approaching its end. His tenderness and spirit of conciliation at the beginning, which left no excuse to the rebels for a resort to arms; his wonderful caution, which did not permit him to pass beyond the sympathy and support of the people; his humaneness which forbade his starving the prisoners of the rebels because they starved ours;--these were qualities which eminently fitted him for the conduct of the war.

But it is more than possible; it is even more than

probable, that just these qualities unfitted him for the final settlement of this conflict. There was danger that he would subordinate his executive functions to his personal sympathies; that he would forget that God had placed the sword of retributive justice in his hands to be used; that he would feel that the traitors had suffered enough already, and needed no further punishment; that he would even pardon Davis and Stephens and Johnston and Lee if they should come into his power. He was drifting in that direction, and most of us were drifting with him.

But, friends, the vindication of this outraged government, and its dignity and safety for the future, demand that treason be judicially punished in the persons of the chief traitors. Treason has not been punished yet; the losses its authors and abettors have suffered have been the natural consequences alone of our own efforts for self-defense. Just and formal punishment demands the conviction of the criminal by due process of law. As the proportions of the rebellion wane the time approaches when retributive justice can execute itself. And it must be that retributive justice be executed, or our conceptions of government and law will become totally debauched.

I say, then, there was danger that the late President, by reason of his kindness of heart, would not be equal to the retributive work which was soon to be required of him; that pardoning the very arch-rebels themselves he would fail to place upon the crime of treason its appropriate stigma, and thus encouraging future rebellion, endanger the future of the republic. If he was in danger of this mistake, then his work was done; and therefore God translated him, having already so nobly done, to glory.

But Andrew Johnson, a man of nerve, has had his heart under the iron heel of this rebellion. He appreciates treason. His sense of justice is paramount to his tender sensibilities. He holds a double-edged and keen-edged sword, which reaches to the southernmost point of Florida. Therefore I believe that God has raised him up to bring this rebellion to the consummation of just retribution. It is not private revenge that he will wreak, but the vengeance of God, whose anointed minister he is. And so God has given him to the nation when the nation needed him. And we will lift our reverent eyes to heaven today, and, gazing through our tears, say, "Thou doest all things well."

Abraham Lincoln's memory will be greener forever that he did the work he did, and finished it when he did. The nation will understand ere long that the dark Providence of last Friday night was a merciful Providence. Andrew Johnson is the Joshua whom God has appointed to consummate the work, which our dead Moses so nobly commenced.

And so, on this Easter Sunday, the anniversary of our Lord's resurrection, we cross the threshold which introduces us as a nation to a career of unexampled victory and puissance and glory. And though the body of our late honored President reposes today in melancholy state, and we weep as we look upon it, yet as Christian men and women we will cry one to another, "Rejoice, for the Lord God omnipotent reigneth; and he will save the people whom he has redeemed with the precious blood of his only Son."

Comforting a Nation

Rev. George D. Boardman
April 19, 1865

AN ADDRESS

IN COMMEMORATION OF

Abraham Lincoln,

PRESIDENT OF THE UNITED STATES,

DELIVERED IN THE MEETING-HOUSE

OF THE

First Baptist Church of Philadelphia,

ON THE DAY OF HIS FUNERAL AT THE NATIONAL CAPITAL,

APRIL 19, 1865.

BY THE

Reverend George Dana Boardman,

PASTOR.

ADDRESS.

How different this scene, my countrymen, from that which was witnessed last Friday morning within these walls!* Then all was gladness and triumph and festal song and gay festoon. Now all is grief and apprehension and requiem and ebon drapery. Why this awful change? Why this universal suspension of business, this awful stillness of the cities and the hamlets? Why, if men appear in the streets, do they walk with slow and measured tread, their hearts failing them through fear, and a grief more crushing than fear? Why from countless spires toll the funereal bells? Why from fort and arsenal and camp and military academy and navy yard and man-of-war mournfully boom the half-hour guns? Why, from the Golden Gate in the far-off West to the St. Croix, aye, to British Newfoundland in the far off East, from every flagstaff and window and balcony and colonnade, from car and engine and steed, float the funereal emblems, fluttering like the ebon wings of countless death-birds? Why this darkness that has fallen on all the land, a darkness so thick that it may be felt? Why this cry that goes up from every hearthstone, a universal, piercing cry, such as there was none ever like it, nor can be like it any more? It is because there is not a house in all the land in which there is not one dead. The nation's Father has been struck down in all his gentle kingliness. And we could almost ask the very sky to quench its too bright sun, and come down to meet our anguish, closing around and enshrouding in its celestial pall the mighty heart that lies so still and cold and dead. O God! Help us to be strong today as we gaze on Abraham Lincoln lying dead on the nation's bier!

I cannot, stricken countrymen, speak long to you today. I trusted, last Sunday, when I gave the announcement for this occasion, that, ere this, I should have regained sway over myself. But in preparing for this solemn hour I have felt the same indescribable stupefaction that I felt on that dreadful Saturday morning. For an hour or two after I read the curdling tale, I felt such a strangeness as I never had felt before, and as I pray God I may never feel again. I felt no anger, not even sadness. I read the awful intelligence over and over and over again; and still it hardly affected me more than if I had never read it at all. And thus an hour or two passed on, in which, like thousands of my countrymen, the soul itself seemed benumbed. And though subsequently the horrible stupefaction passed away, to be succeeded by most poignant bitterness of soul, yet, in endeavoring to arrange my thoughts for this dreaded occasion, I have felt the same stupefying, freezing horror creeping over me again. It seems to me that brain, heart, pen, are paralyzed. Instead of attempting to say aught today, I feel like escaping from the presence of my fellow men into some secluded forest-dell, where I may breathe out a sorrow too sacred for words. All I can do is to bring the briefest tribute, and reverently lay it, amidst the dew of your tears, at the feet of the mighty dead.

Abraham Lincoln was born of respectable parentage in Kentucky, February 12, 1809. In 1816, his parents removed to Indiana, where in their new home Abraham spent the next ten years in hard manual labor on his father's farm. The only school education which he ever received was that which he obtained at intervals during this time, amounting in the aggregate to about a year. In 1830 he removed with his father to Illinois, and in the following year was employed as one of the hands in navigating a flatboat down the Mississippi to New Orleans. On the breaking out of the Black Hawk war, in 1832, he served his country for three months as the captain of a volunteer company. On his return he began the study of law, to which he devoted himself with most persistent assiduity. In 1834 he was elected to the legislature by the highest vote cast for any candidate in the State, which position he held for six years in virtue of consecutive re-elections. Meanwhile he had removed to the capital of the State, where he rapidly rose to great distinction as an advocate in jury trials. In 1846, at the age of 37, Illinois sent him as one of her representatives at Washington.

His Congressional career was marked by a scrupulous devotion to the duties of his office, by an inflexible adherence to principle, by a generous, intelligent sympathy with all measures of reform, among which I may particularly mention the resolution which he offered, on

January 16, 1849, for the abolition of slavery in the District of Columbia, on what he conceived to be a constitutional basis. After the expiration of his Congressional term, he applied himself ardently to his profession till that dark deed, the Repeal of the Missouri Compromise, called him again into the political arena. He was immediately acknowledged as one of the most prominent political leaders in the State. In 1858 he was unanimously nominated by his party as candidate for United States Senator in opposition to Judge Douglas. You have not forgotten how these two remarkable men canvassed the State together, with what extraordinary ability and courtesy the debate was conducted on both sides, and how profound an interest the canvass excited throughout the Union. The result of this contest was, that though Mr. Lincoln received a popular majority of four thousand votes, yet Mr. Douglas was elected Senator by the joint ballot of the legislature. On May 18, 1860, he was unanimously nominated by the Republican National Convention a candidate for President, which nomination was ratified by the people on November 6, and, on the 4th of March, 1861, having succeeded in reaching Washington in spite of the most desperate obstacles to prevent it, was inaugurated the sixteenth President of the United States. At twenty minutes past four o'clock on the morning of April 12, 1861, the grand conspiracy inaugurated civil war in America by opening the fire of one hundred and forty guns on Fort Sumter, Major Robert Anderson commanding. Who needs to have the tale, henceforth so harrowing, repeated? It is enough to think of the dead President, without dwelling on the intervening years of mingled woe and glory. One event, indeed, must be specialized; for it overtops all the other great events of this unparalleled epoch, as towered the Olympian Jove above the lesser gods of the Grecian heaven. Your own swelling hearts have anticipated me when I tell you that it was the Emancipation Proclamation of January 1st, 1863. Without particularizing further, it is enough to say, that in the terrific and long-continued tornado which burst upon the country on the bombardment of Sumter, whenever the ship of state plunged most wildly amidst the engulfing billows, or grated most heavily on the foundering reefs, or echoed most hoarsely with the shrieks of the despairing, one man there was who ever walked her deck with quiet intrepidity, his great heart ever true and trustful, his clear brain ever vigilant and wide-sweeping, his strong hand ever untrembling, towering, placid and imperial, like Neptune's brow, above the white foam, and smiling it into peace. After a canvass of unexampled intensity, throughout which he preserved the same calm beauty of soul, he was, on the 8th of November, 1864, re-elected President of the United States by an almost unprecedented electoral majority; and on the 4th of March, 1865, he reassumed the executive functions in an Inaugural of most impressive yet gentlest majesty. On the 14th of April, 1865, the national flag was by his command re-uplifted on the ramparts of Sumter, as a symbol of the re-establishment of the national sovereignty throughout the Republic; and on the evening of that memorable day the kingliest man that ever breathed the air of the Western hemisphere was laid low by a bullet thrice accursed, for it was sped by an assassin, a traitor, and a slavery worshipper.

Such, in briefest terms, is an outline of the career of America's foremost son. What more can be said as we gather in tearful reverence around his bier? Without distinction of lineage, he gained a distinction, which no lineage could give. Born among and as one of the common people, he ever retained, amidst a courtliness of power, which European dynasties a thousand years old might envy, a fellow feeling with the common people, by his own inherent greatness rising to be their type aggregate, embodiment, and symbol. But passing over those years of boyish poverty and struggle, and also the years of youthful brain and will endeavor, and conquest too, let us gaze on him when, in the maturity of his powers, he wields a scepter more august than that of Roman Caesar. It is difficult to form a just estimate of his character; for, its vast proportions are lost in its extraordinary symmetry. For, as in entering for the first time St. Peter's basilica at Rome, you are disappointed, because the grandeur of outline is melted and lost in the exquisite adaptation of detail, so to the thoughtless observer the character of the late President seems less great than it really was, because lost in its perfect equipoise and rounded globe. But let us proceed with our attempt at delineation. The historian to be born a hundred years hence will, I judge, say of Abraham Lincoln something as follows.

He was not a man lustrously brilliant in any one direction. No one faculty of brain markedly towered over another. But he was none the less great in that his greatness was so rounded, having less the transient dazzle of the meteor than the steady quiet sparkle of the fixed star. His logic was intuitive rather than tentative, instinctive rather than elaborative. He was wont to come to his conclusions less by the laborious rowings of his reason than by the unconscious floatings of his instinctive, inborn shrewdness and sagacity. Hence the facility with which he detected the pivotal point in any question, however complex. Hence the ease and precision with which he led the people to catch the same point, leading them directly thither by the avenue of a diction which, however peculiar and homely, was as straightforward and pellucid as his own judgment. Hence, also, it was that he so rarely made mistakes. Hence it was that every public act or plan of his, however wide-spread or intense the execration with which it was first received, was sure, sooner or later, to win the applauding verdict of the people. Guided thus by a system of well-nigh infallible instincts, by which he knew what he ought to do, and when to do it, and how to do it, he might well have taken as his own motto the heraldic bearing of the Earl of Buckinghamshire, Nulla vestigia retrorsum.

But because the intellect of the late President was intuitive rather than ratiocinative, it does not follow that he was not intellectually great; for as, according to the profounder theologians, the intuitive John was greater than the syllogistic Paul, so it seems to me, that Mr. Lincoln, intellectually surveyed, stands in the very first rank of those who have, in either hemisphere, wielded the scepter. He had an unusually comprehensive mind, taking in at a glance all the aspects of the most many-sided question, almost always coming unerringly to a conclusion, when an inferior and less spherical mind would have been puzzled and paralyzed by a seeming contradiction, as, for instance, when social or a political necessity is balanced by a legal or constitutional difficulty, or when a pressing moral obligation is offset by a present practical impossibility. Seeing all sides of a question, and intuitively just, he was enabled to equate the problem, thus steering the ship of state safely between the Charybdis of fanatic propulsion and the Scylla of timorous procrastination. The highest eulogy that can be pronounced on the intellectual character of a ruler, in times of great civil convulsion, is that it is his policy to have no policy, content with keeping his ship trim as he permits her to sweep downwards with the precipitous torrent. That eulogy the late President deserves beyond any ruler the world has seen.

And yet Mr. Lincoln was not wanting in executive force. Because he made no pretensions to special firmness, and vaunted not his purposes, people at first imagined that he was irresolute. But as time rolled on we began to see that beneath that mild, unassuming exterior lay an imperial will, that serenely swayed all who came in contact with him, however high in the military or executive councils of the nation they stood; and yet so quiet was this sway that they hardly knew that the scepter was over them. Observe the modest assurance with which he rules the Secretary of State and the Lieutenant General, placidly reserving to himself every ultimate responsibility. Nor was his inflexibility less than his force. All the powers of earth could not drive him to take a step till he thought it was right; and when convinced that it was right, all the powers of earth could not prevent his taking it. And all this, too, was without the slightest ostentation. Like a wire-bridge across a mountain gorge, he could sway to the softest zephyr, yet, like the same wire-bridge, the whirlwind could not uproot him.

Gifted with this intellectual judgment so instinctively infallible, and this gentle steadfastness of will, the late President blended with it a moral nature remarkably pure, keen, sensitive, and controlling. He was the very soul of integrity. It were as much as a man's liberty, certainly more than his expectations, were worth, to enter the presence of Abraham Lincoln with either flattery, threat, or bribe. Himself as transparent as crystal, he loathed whatever was refractive or opaque. He was absolutely incorruptible. Shrewd beyond most men, his shrewdness was the clear, piercing vision of a clean, single heart, that knew not how to

> Spread its sails
> With 'vantage to the gale of others' passions.

Conscious of personal integrity, self-reliant, constitutionally genial, having an abiding faith in the instinct and persistence of the people as a corporate whole, assured of the justice of the majestic cause, and having a deep confidence in the overruling and merciful God, he was enabled to retain, in hours of darkest gloom, a cheerfulness of spirit, which often found vent in broadest and most grotesque humors. I doubt not that this constitutional blithesomeness of soul was one of the elements which contributed to the preservation of his life beneath the most crushing responsibilities that ever fell on man. And amidst all these distracting, hardening, shriveling cares, he ever retained the same freshness and tenderness of soul. While just and kind to all, he was, to the very last, in a special sense, the poor man's friend. And among all those who weep over his untimely death, the chief mourners of the land, next to the members of his own family, are the sable millions whom his own hand had set free. I honestly believe that there never trod the earth a more sympathetic, unselfish, large-hearted, forgiving man than he. Whatever filled up the vast circumference of that soul, the thought of Abraham Lincoln's own self was no occupant of it. By one of those spontaneous consents of the people, which spring up only on the soil of truth, he was instinctively styled Father Abraham. He was indeed the father of the whole American people, from the St. Lawrence to the Mexican Gulf, and he lived only in his children. For them, east and west, north and south, loyal and insurgent, he lived, and prayed, and schemed, and toiled, taxing every power of his clear and comprehending brain, and every sensibility of his delicate and boundless heart. I know not whether he was a Christian. The All-seeing alone knows that. Accounts, however, of his devotional habits have occasionally reached us too well authenticated to be set aside. Certainly he had a deep and abiding sense of the holy authority of God, and an inspiring confidence in His merciful providence. I could have wished, indeed, that since he must fall, he had fallen elsewhere, engaged in a purer service, which had some "relish of salvation in't." But let that glide into oblivion. It is the solitary cloud that flecked the expanse of his public career.

If every mortal obeyed Wolsey's dying counsel, it was Abraham Lincoln:

Cromwell! I charge thee fling away ambition;
By that sin fell the angels; how can man, then,
The image of his Maker, hope to win by 't?
Love thyself last; cherish those hearts that hate thee;
Corruption wins not more than honesty.
Still in thy right hand carry gentle peace,
To silence envious tongues. Be just, and fear not!

Let all the ends thou aim'st at be thy Country's,
Thy God's and Truth's!
Then, if thou fall'st, O Cromwell!
Thou fall'st a blessed martyr!

And this is the man so augustly rich in the elements of an exalted manhood, who has suddenly been stricken down, not by an adventurous invader from a foreign soil, seeking to avenge his own nationality; not by a reckless highwayman, who must needs replenish his empty purse; not by a staggering madman, crazed by his potations; but by an American desperado, who, whether the appointed and duly certified organ of conspirators or not, it matters little, is nevertheless the actual summation and type of that slaveholding power, which, rather than lose its grasp on the sable chattels made in God's image, after His likeness, has been willing to drench a continent in fratricidal blood. Oh, what a type and symbol of this whole insurrectionary movement of the South, this assassination of President Lincoln has been! If ever the genius of suicide took upon itself the impersonation of a human form, it was when this colossal slaveholding conspiracy was epitomized and became incarnate in the person of the diabolical miscreant, whose only passport to immortality is, that, when the martyr President fell, his descending shadow fell on him, and set his name in blackness of darkness forever more. And yet, were a merciful Omnipotence to restore to life the dead President, I doubt not that though some of us may at first have interpreted the voice of his blood, like that of the world's first martyr by the gates of Eden, as a cry for vengeance, yet, when those gentle lips moved again, we should hear a voice, which, like the sweet cadence that softly billowed the air on the first Good Friday, speaketh better things than that of Abel. And I believe that even today there are thousands of penitent ones in those desolated Southern homes, whose rebellious pride has been subdued by this awful parricide, and who, were the privilege allowed them, would come and

Kiss dead Caesar's wounds,
And dip their napkins in his sacred blood;
Yea, beg a hair of him for memory,
And, dying, mention it within their wills,
Bequeathing it as richest legacy
Unto their issue.

Yes, it shall be said of the martyred President as was said three thousand years ago of the grand old Hebrew judge and patriot, "The dead which he slew at his death were more than they which he slew in his life."

My countrymen! I have woven my garland, simple and unworthy as it is, and hung it on the bier. It is scarce fitting to linger longer. For even now the sad cortege has begun to move which shall bear to his last sleeping-place all that is mortal of the martyr statesman, patriot, emancipator, and friend. And as in the days of King Joash, when the

Comforting a Nation

body of the dead Israelite, on being let down into the sepulcher of Elisha, and on touching the bones of the mighty prophet, was revived and stood on its feet again, so may God grant that as the nation's dead heart reverently touches today the dead heart of the great patriot, it may be quickened into life again, and stand before the astonished nations in all the strength and splendor of a new-born majesty!

Yes! Move on in majestic state to thy Illinois tomb, amidst the bowing ranks of a weeping nation, thou illustrious martyr for us all! Thy dead, murdered corpse is the watchword, and, with God's grace, the victor paean of an emancipated, chastened, glorified Republic!

Rev. Matthew Simpson
The burial May 4, 1865

Methodist Bishop Matthew Simpson moved from Ohio to Evanston, Illinois in 1859. Simpson got to know President-elect Lincoln in the winter of 1860-61 when he visited with him in Springfield in search of support for Northwestern University.

When President-elect Lincoln left Springfield for Washington, the bishop was in the crowd at the railroad station. After the outbreak of the Civil War Bishop Simpson rushed to Washington. The President "received him cordially," wrote biographer Robert D. Clark.

FUNERAL ADDRESS

Delivered at the Burial of

PRESIDENT LINCOLN,

AT SPRINGFIELD, ILLINOIS,
MAY 4, 1865.

By Rev. MATTHEW SIMPSON, D.D.,
ONE OF THE BISHOPS OF THE METHODIST EPISCOPAL CHURCH.

FUNERAL ADDRESS.
FELLOW-CITIZENS OF ILLINOIS, AND OF MANY PARTS OF OUR ENTIRE UNION:

Near the capitol of this large and growing State of Illinois, in the midst of this beautiful grove, and at the open mouth of the vault which has just received the remains of our fallen chieftain, we gather to pay a tribute of respect and to drop the tears of sorrow around the ashes of the mighty dead. A little more than four years ago he left his plain and quiet home in yonder city, receiving the parting words of the concourse of friends who in the midst of the dropping of the gentle shower gathered around him. He spoke of the pain of parting from the place where he had lived for a quarter of a century, where his children had been born and his home had been rendered pleasant by friendly associations; and, as he left, he made an earnest request, in the hearing of some who are present at this hour, that, as he was about to enter upon responsibilities which he believed to be greater than any which had fallen upon any man since the days of Washington, the people would offer up prayers that God would aid and sustain him in the work which they had given him to do. His company left your quiet city, but as it went snares were in waiting for the chief magistrate. Scarcely did he escape the dangers of the way or the hands of the assassin as he neared Washington; and I believe he escaped only through the vigilance of officers and the prayers of the people, so that the blow was suspended for more than four years, which was at last permitted, through the providence of God, to fall.

How different the occasion which witnessed his departure from that which witnessed his return! Doubtless you expected to take him by the hand, and to feel the warm grasp which you had felt in other days, and to see the tall form walking among you which you had delighted to honor in years past. But he was never permitted to come until he came with lips mute and silent, the frame encoffined, and a weeping nation following as his mourners. Such a scene as his return to you was never witnessed. Among the events of history there have been great processions of mourners. There was one for the patriarch Jacob, which went up from Egypt, and the Egyptians wondered at the evidences of reverence and filial affection which came from the hearts of the Israelites. There was mourning when Moses fell upon the heights of Pisgah, and was hid from human view. There have been mourning's in the kingdoms of the earth when kings and warriors have fallen. But never was there in the history of man such mourning as that which has accompanied this funeral procession, and has gathered around the mortal remains of him who was our loved one, and who now sleeps among us. If we glance at the procession which followed him, we see how the nation stood aghast.

Tears filled the eyes of manly, sun-burnt faces.

Strong men, as they clasped the hands of their friends, were not able in words to find vent for their grief. Women and little children caught up the tidings as they ran through the land, and were melted into tears. The nation stood still. Men left their plows in the fields and asked what the end should be. The hum of manufactories ceased, and the sound of the hammer was not heard. Busy merchants closed their doors, and in the exchange gold passed no more from hand to hand. Though three weeks have elapsed, the nation has scarcely breathed easily yet. A mournful silence is abroad upon the land; nor is this mourning confined to any class or to any district of country. Men of all political parties, and of all religious creeds, have united in paying this mournful tribute. The archbishop of the Roman Catholic Church in New York and a Protestant minister walked side by side in the sad procession, and a Jewish rabbi performed a part of the solemn services.

Here are gathered around his tomb the representatives of the army and navy, senators, judges, governors, and officers of all the branches of the government. Here, too, are members of civic processions, with men and women from the humblest as well as the highest occupations. Here and there, too, are tears as sincere and warm as any that drop, which come from the eyes of those whose kindred and whose race have been freed from their chains by him whom they mourn as their deliverer. More persons have gazed on the face of the departed than ever looked upon the face of any other departed man. More have looked on the procession for sixteen hundred miles, by night and by day, by sunlight, dawn, twilight, and by torchlight, than ever before watched the progress of a procession.

We ask why this wonderful mourning, this great procession? I answer, first, a part of the interest has arisen from the times in which we live, and in which he that has fallen was a principal actor. It is a principle of our nature that feelings once excited turn readily from the object by which they are excited to some other object which may for the time being take possession of the mind. Another principle is, the deepest affections of our hearts gather around some human form in which are incarnated the living thoughts and ideas of the passing age. If we look then at the times, we see an age of excitement. For four years the popular heart has been stirred to its inmost depth. War had come upon us, dividing families, separating nearest and dearest friends, a war the extent and magnitude of which no one could estimate; a war in which the blood of brethren was shed by a brother's hand. A call for soldiers was made by this voice now hushed, and all over the land, from hill to mountain, from plain to valley, there sprung up thousands of bold hearts, ready to go forth and save our national Union. This feeling of excitement was transformed next into a feeling of deep grief because of the dangers in which our country was placed. Many said, "Is it possible to save our nation?" Some in our country, and nearly all the leading men in other countries, declared it to be impossible to maintain the Union; and many an honest and patriotic heart was deeply pained with apprehensions of common ruin; and many, in grief and almost in despair, anxiously inquired, What shall the end of these things be? In addition to this wives had given their husbands, mothers their sons, the pride and joy of their hearts. They saw them put on the uniform, they saw them take the martial step, and they tried to hide their deep feeling of sadness. Many dear ones slept upon the battlefield never to return again, and there was mourning in every mansion and in every cabin in our broad land. Then came a feeling of deeper sadness as the story came of prisoners tortured to death or starved through the mandates of those who are called the representatives of the chivalry, and who claimed to be the honorable ones of the earth; and as we read the stories of frames attenuated and reduced to mere skeletons, our grief turned partly into horror and partly into a cry for vengeance.

Then this feeling was changed to one of joy. There came signs of the end of this rebellion. We followed the career of our glorious generals. We saw our army, under the command of the brave officer who is guiding this procession, climb up the heights of Lookout Mountain, and drive the rebels from their strongholds. Another brave general swept through Georgia, South and North Carolina, and drove the combined armies of the rebels before him, while the honored Lieutenant General held Lee and his hosts in a death-grasp.

Then the tidings came that Richmond was evacuated, and that Lee had surrendered. The bells rang merrily all over the land. The booming of cannon was heard; illuminations and torchlight processions manifested the general joy, and families were looking for the speedy return of their loved ones from the field of battle. Just in the midst of this wildest joy, in one hour, nay, in one moment, the tidings thrilled throughout the land that Abraham Lincoln, the best of presidents, had perished by the hands of an assassin. Then all the feelings which had been gathering for four years in forms of excitement, grief, horror, and joy, turned into one wail of woe, a sadness inexpressible, an anguish unutterable.

But it is not the times merely, which caused this mourning. The mode of his death must be taken into the account. Had he died on a bed of illness, with kind friends around him; had the sweat of death been wiped from his brow by gentle hands, while he was yet conscious; could he have had power to speak words of affection to his stricken widow, or words of counsel to us like those which we heard in his parting inaugural at Washington, which shall now be immortal, how it would have softened or assuaged something of the grief! There might at least have been preparation for the event. But no moment of warning was given to him or to us. He was stricken down, too, when his hopes for the end of the rebellion were bright, and prospects of a joyous life were before him. There was a cabinet meeting that day, said to have been the most cheerful and happy of any held since the beginning of the rebellion. After this meeting he talked with his friends, and spoke of the four years of tempest, of the storm being over, and of the four years of pleasure and joy now awaiting him, as the weight of care and anxiety would be taken from his mind, and he could have happy days with his family again. In the midst of these anticipations he left his house never to return alive. The evening was Good Friday, the saddest day in the whole calendar for the Christian Church, henceforth in this country to be made sadder, if possible by the memory of our nation's loss; and so filled with grief was every Christian heart that even all the joyous thought of Easter Sunday failed to remove the crushing sorrow under which the true worshiper bowed in the house of God.

But the great cause of this mourning is to be found

in the man himself. Mr. Lincoln was no ordinary man. I believe the conviction has been growing on the nation's mind, as it certainly has been on my own, especially in the last years of his administration, that by the hand of God he was especially singled out to guide our government in these troublesome times, and it seems to me that the hand of God may be traced in many of the events connected with his history. First, then, I recognize this in the physical education, which he received, and which prepared him for enduring herculean labors. In the foils of his boyhood and the labors of his manhood, God was giving him an iron frame. Next to this was his identification with the heart of the great people, understanding their feelings because he was one of them, and connected with them in their movements and life. His education was simple. A few months spent in the schoolhouse gave him the elements of education. He read few books, but mastered all he read. Pilgrim's Progress, Aesop's Fables, and the Life of Washington, were his favorites. In these we recognize the works which gave the bias to his character, and which partly molded his style. His early life, with its varied struggles, joined him indissolubly to the working masses, and no elevation in society diminished his respect for the sons of toil. He knew what it was to fell the tall trees of the forest and to stem the current of the broad Mississippi. His home was in the growing west, the heart of the republic and, invigorated by the wind, which swept over its prairies, he learned lessons of self-reliance, which sustained him in seasons of adversity.

His genius was soon recognized, as true genius always will be, and he was placed in the legislature of his state. Already acquainted with the principles of law, he devoted his thoughts to matters of public interest, and began to be looked on as the coming statesman. As early as 1839 he presented resolutions in the legislature asking for emancipation in the District of Columbia, when, with but rare exceptions, the whole popular mind of his state was opposed to the measure. From that hour he was a steady and uniform friend of humanity, and was preparing for the conflict of later years.

If you ask me on what mental characteristic his greatness rested, I answer, On a quick and ready perception of facts; on a memory, unusually tenacious and retentive; and on a logical turn of mind, which followed sternly and unwaveringly every link in the chain of thought on every subject which he was called to investigate. I think there have been minds more broad in their character, more comprehensive in their scope, but I doubt if ever there has been a man who could follow step by step, with more logical power, the points which he desired to illustrate. He gained this power by the close study of geometry, and by a determination to perceive the truth in all its relations and simplicity, and when found, to utter it.

It is said of him that in childhood when he had any difficulty in listening to a conversation, to ascertain what people meant, if he retired to rest he could not sleep till he tried to understand the precise point intended, and when understood, to frame language to convey in it a clearer manner to others. Who that has read his messages fails to perceive the directness and the simplicity of his style? And this very trait, which was scoffed at and decried by opponents, is now recognized as one of the strong points of that mighty mind which has so powerfully influenced the destiny of this nation, and which shall, for ages to come, influence the destiny of humanity.

It was not, however, chiefly by his mental faculties that he gained such control over mankind. His moral power gave him pre-eminence. The convictions of men that Abraham Lincoln was an honest man led them to yield to his guidance. As has been said of Cobden, whom he greatly resembled, he made all men feel a sense of himself; a recognition of individuality; a self-relying power. They saw in him a man whom they believed would do what is right, regardless of all consequences. It was this moral feeling, which gave him the greatest, hold on the people, and made his utterances almost oracular. When the nation was angered by the perfidy of foreign nations in allowing privateers to be fitted out, he uttered the significant expression, "One war at a time," and it stilled the national heart. When his own friends were divided as to what steps should be taken as to slavery, that simple utterance, "I will save the Union, if I can, with slavery; if not, slavery must perish, for the Union must be preserved," became the rallying word. Men felt the struggle was for the Union, and all other questions must be subsidiary.

But after all, by the acts of a man shall his fame be perpetuated. What are his acts? Much praise is due to the men who aided him. He called able counselors around him; some of whom have displayed the highest order of talent united with the purest and most devoted patriotism. He summoned able generals into the field, men who have borne the sword as bravely as ever any human arm has borne it. He had the aid of prayerful and thoughtful men everywhere. But, under his guiding hands, wise counsels were combined and great movements conducted.

Turn toward the different departments. We had an unorganized militia, a mere skeleton army, yet, under his care, that army has been enlarged into a force, which, for skill, intelligence, efficiency, and bravery, surpasses any, which the world had ever seen. Before its veterans the fame of even the renowned veterans of Napoleon shall pale, and the mothers and sisters on these hillsides, and all over the land, shall take to their arms again braver sons and brothers than ever fought in European wars. The reason is obvious. Money, or a desire for fame, collected those armies, or they were rallied to sustain favorite thrones or dynasties; but the armies he called into being fought for liberty, for the Union, and for the right of self-government; and many of them felt that the battles they won were for humanity everywhere, and for all time; for I believe that God has not suffered this terrible rebellion to come upon our land merely for a chastisement to us, or as a lesson to our age.

There are moments which involve in themselves eternities. There are instants, which seem to contain germs, which shall develop, and bloom forever. Such a moment came in the tide of time to our land, when a question must be settled which affected all the earth. The contest was for human freedom, not for this republic merely, not for the Union simply, but to decide whether the people, as a people, in their entire majesty, were destined to be the government, or whether they were to be subjects to tyrants or aristocrats, or to class-rule of any kind. This is the great question, for which we have been fighting, and its decision is at hand, and the result of the contest will affect the ages to come. If successful, republics will spread, in spite of monarchs, all over this earth.

I turn from the army to the navy. What was it when the war commenced? Now we have our ships-of-war at home and abroad, to guard privateers in foreign sympathizing ports, as well as to care for every part of our own coast. They have taken forts that military men said could not be taken; and a brave admiral, for the first time in the world's history, lashed himself to the mast, there to remain as long as he had a particle of skill or strength to watch over his ship, while it engaged in the perilous contest of taking the strong forts of the rebels.

Then again I turn to the treasury department. Where should the money come from? Wise men predicted ruin, but our national credit has been maintained, and our currency is safer today than it ever was before. Not only so, but through our national bonds, if properly used, we shall have a permanent basis for our currency, and an investment so desirable for capitalists of other nations that, under the laws of trade, I believe the center of exchange will speedily be transferred from England to the United States.

But the great act of the mighty chieftain, on which his fame shall rest long after his frame shall molder away, is that of giving freedom to a race. We have all been taught to revere the sacred characters. Among them Moses stands pre-eminently high. He received the law from God, and his name is honored among the hosts of heaven. Was not his greatest act the delivering of three millions of his kindred out of bondage? Yet we may assert that Abraham Lincoln, by his proclamation, liberated more enslaved people than ever Moses set free, and those not of his kindred or his race. Such a power, or such an opportunity, God has seldom given to man. When other events shall have been forgotten; when this world shall have become a network of republics;

when every throne shall be swept from the face of the earth; when literature shall enlighten all minds; when the claims of humanity shall be recognized everywhere, this act shall still be conspicuous on the pages of history. We are thankful that God gave to Abraham Lincoln the decision and wisdom and grace to issue that proclamation, which stands high above all other papers, which have been penned by uninspired men.

Abraham Lincoln was a good man. He was known as an honest, temperate, forgiving man; a just man; a man of noble heart in every way. As to his religious experience, I cannot speak definitely, because I was not privileged to know much of his private sentiments. My acquaintance with him did not give me the opportunity to hear him speak on those topics. This I know, however, he read the Bible frequently; loved it for its great truths and its profound teachings; and he tried to be guided by its precepts. He believed in Christ the Saviour of sinners; and I think he was sincere in trying to bring his life into harmony with the principles of revealed religion. Certainly if there ever was a man who illustrated some of the principles of pure religion, that man was our departed president. Look over all his speeches; listen to his utterances. He never spoke unkindly of any man. Even the rebels received no word of anger from him; and his last day illustrated in a remarkable manner his forgiving disposition. A dispatch was received that afternoon that Thompson and Tucker were trying to make their escape through Maine, and it was proposed to arrest them. Mr. Lincoln, however, preferred rather to let them quietly escape. He was seeking to save the very men who had been plotting his destruction. This morning we read a proclamation offering $25,000 for the arrest of these men as aiders and abettors of his assassination; so that, in his expiring acts, he was saying, "Father, forgive them, they know not what they do."

As a ruler I doubt if any president has ever shown such trust in God, or in public documents so frequently referred to Divine aid. Often did he remark to friends and to delegations that his hope for our success rested in his conviction that God would bless our efforts, because we were trying to do right. To the address of a large religious body he replied, "Thanks be unto God, who, in our national trials, giveth us the Churches." To a minister who said he hoped the Lord was on our side, he replied that it gave him no concern whether the Lord was on our side or not "For," he added, "I know the Lord is always on the side of right;" and with deep feeling added, "But God is my witness that it is my constant anxiety and prayer that both myself and this nation should be on the Lord's side."

In his domestic life he was exceedingly kind and affectionate. He was a devoted husband and father. During his presidential term he lost his second son, Willie. To an officer of the army he said, not long since, "Do you ever find yourself talking with the dead?" and added, "Since Willie's death I catch myself every day involuntarily talking with him, as if he were with me." On his widow, who is unable to be here, I need only invoke the blessing of Almighty God that she may be comforted and sustained. For his son, who has witnessed the exercises of this hour, all that I can desire is that the mantle of his father may fall upon him.

Let us pause a moment in the lesson of the hour before we part. This man, though he fell by an assassin, still fell under the permissive hand of God. He had some wise purpose in allowing him so to fall. What more could he have desired of life for himself? Were not his honors full? There was no office to which he could aspire. The popular heart clung around him as around no other man. The nations of the world had learned to honor our chief magistrate. If rumors of a desired alliance with England be true, Napoleon trembled when he heard of the fall of Richmond, and asked what nation would join him to protect him against our government under the guidance of such a man. His fame was full, his work was done, and he sealed his glory by becoming the nation's great martyr for liberty.

He appears to have had a strange presentiment, early in political life, that some day he would be president. You see it indicated in 1839. Of the slave power he said, "Broken by it I too may be;

bow to it I never will. The probability that we may fail in the struggle ought not to deter us from the support of a cause, which I deem to be just. It shall not deter me. If ever I feel the soul within me elevate and expand to those dimensions not wholly unworthy of its Almighty architect, it is when I contemplate the cause of my country, deserted by all the world besides, and I standing up boldly and alone, and hurling defiance at her victorious oppressors. Here, without contemplating consequences, before high Heaven, and in the face of the world, I swear eternal fidelity to the just cause, as I deem it, of the land of my life, my liberty, and my love." And yet, recently, he said to more than one, "I never shall live out the four years of my term. When the rebellion is crushed my work is done." So it was. He lived to see the last battle fought, and dictate a dispatch from the home of Jefferson Davis; lived till the power of the rebellion was broken; and then having done the work for which God had sent him, angels, I trust, were sent to shield him from one moment of pain or suffering, and to bear him from this world to the high and glorious realm where the patriot and the good shall live forever.

His career teaches young men that every position of eminence is open before the diligent and the worthy. To the active men of the country his example is an incentive to trust in God and do right. To the ambitious there is this fearful lesson: Of the four candidates for presidential honors in 1860, two of them--Douglas and Lincoln--once competitors, but now sleeping patriots, rest from their labors; Bell abandoned to perish in poverty and misery, as a traitor might perish; and Breckinridge is a frightened fugitive, with the brand of traitor on his brow.

Standing, as, we do today, by his coffin and his sepulcher let us resolve to carry forward the policy which he so nobly begun. Let us do right to all men. Let us vow, in the sight of Heaven, to eradicate every vestige of human slavery; to give every human being his true position before God and man; to crush every form of rebellion, and to stand by the flag which God has given us. How joyful that it floated over parts of every state before Mr. Lincoln's career was ended! How singular that, to the fact of the assassin's heels being caught in the folds of the flag, we are probably indebted for his capture. The flag and the traitor must ever be enemies.

Traitors will probably suffer by the change of rulers, for one of sterner mould, and who himself has deeply suffered from the rebellion, now wields the sword of justice. Our country, too, is stronger for the trial. A republic was declared by monarchists too weak to endure a civil war; yet we have crushed the most gigantic rebellion in history, and have grown in strength and population every year of the struggle. We have passed through the ordeal of a popular election while swords and bayonets were in the field, and have come out unharmed. And now, in an hour of excitement, with a large minority having preferred another man for President, when the bullet of the assassin has laid our President prostrate, has there been a mutiny? Has any rival proffered his claims? Out of an army of near a million, no officer or soldier uttered one note of dissent; and, in an hour or two after Mr. Lincoln's death, another leader, under constitutional forms, occupied his chair, and the government moved forward without one single jar. The world will learn that republics are the strongest governments on earth.

And now, my friends, in the words of the departed, "with malice toward none," free from all feelings of personal vengeance, yet believing that the sword must not be borne in vain, let us go forward even in painful duty. Let every man who was a senator or representative in Congress, and who aided in beginning this rebellion, and thus led to the slaughter of our sons and daughters; be brought to speedy and to certain punishment. Let every officer educated at the public expense, and who, having been advanced to high position, perjured himself and turned his sword against the vitals of his country, be doomed to a traitor's death. This, I believe, is the will of the American people. Men may attempt to compromise, and to restore these traitors and murderers to society again. Vainly may they talk of the fancied honor or chivalry of these murderers of our sons--these starvers of our prisoners--these officers who mined their prisons and placed kegs of powder to destroy our captive officers. But the American people will rise in their majesty and sweep all such compromises and compromisers away, and will declare that there shall be no safety for rebel leaders. But to the deluded masses we will extend the arms of forgiveness. We will take them to our hearts, and walk with them side by side, as we go forward to work out a glorious destiny.

The time will come when, in the beautiful words of him whose lips are now forever sealed, "The mystic cords of memory, stretching from every battlefield and patriot grave to every living heart and hearthstone all over this broad land, will yet swell the chorus of the Union, when again touched, as surely they will be, by the better angels of our nature."

Chieftain, farewell! The nation mourns thee. Mothers shall teach thy name to their lisping children. The youth of our land shall emulate thy virtues. Statesmen shall study thy record and learn lessons of wisdom. Mute though thy lips be, yet they still speak. Hushed is thy voice, but its echoes of liberty are ringing through the world, and the sons of bondage listen with joy. Prisoned thou art in death, and yet thou art marching abroad, and chains and manacles are bursting at thy touch. Thou didst fall not for thyself. The assassin had no hate for thee. Our hearts were aimed at, our national life was sought. We crown thee as our martyr, and humanity enthrones thee as her triumphant son. Hero, Martyr, Friend, FAREWELL!

A COLLECTION OF SERMONS

THE TOMB
BY LARRY TOLLER

Rest O Abraham
Rest O freedom's soldier
Weary from your work
Many pass in solemn walk
On each mind and heart
Your image firmly planted

Rest O gentle giant
There can be no one like you
With wit and wisdom
Heart and soul
Your work is ever new

Rest O Abraham
Freedom's song must never end
New choruses added day by day
We must never forget
The terrible price you paid

After his death in 1865, Abraham Lincoln's Illinois friends worked to gain permission to bury him in his hometown of Springfield, IL.

The tomb was dedicated in 1874.

The 117-foot tall granite tomb contains the bodies of Lincoln, his wife Mary, and three of his four sons -- Edward, William and Thomas (Tad). Robert, the oldest son, planned to be buried in this tomb with his parents and brothers but instead was buried in Arlington National Cemetery.

A Collection of Sermons